Graphic Medieval History

THE DARK AGES
AND THE Vikings

By Gary Jeffrey & Illustrated by Nick Spender

Crabtree Publishing Company
www.crabtreebooks.com

Crabtree Publishing Company
www.crabtreebooks.com
1-800-387-7650

Publishing in Canada
616 Welland Ave.
St. Catharines, ON
L2M 5V6

Published in the United States
PMB 59051, 350 Fifth Ave.
59th Floor,
New York, NY 10118

Published in **2014 by CRABTREE PUBLISHING COMPANY.**

Printed in Canada/032014/MA20140124

Created and produced by:

David West Children's Books

Project development, design, and concept:

David West Children's Books

Author and designer: Gary Jeffrey

Illustrator: Nick Spender

Editor: Kathy Middleton

Proofreader: Adrianna Morganelli

Production coordinator and Prepress technician:

Ken Wright

Print coordinator:

Margaret Amy Salter

Photo credits:

p5 middle, Uwe kils

Library and Archives Canada Cataloguing in Publication

Jeffrey, Gary, author
The dark ages and the Vikings / Gary Jeffrey ; illustrator: Nick Spender.

(Graphic medieval history)
Includes index.
Issued in print and electronic formats.
ISBN 978-0-7787-0401-0 (bound).--ISBN 978-0-7787-0407-2 (pbk.).--
ISBN 978-1-4271-7513-7 (html).--ISBN 978-1-4271-7519-9 (pdf)

1. Vikings--Great Britain--Juvenile literature. 2. Great Britain--History--Anglo-Saxon period, 449-1066--Juvenile literature. 3. Vikings--Great Britain--Comic books, strips, etc. 4. Great Britain--History--Anglo-Saxon period, 449-1066--Comic books, strips, etc. 5. Graphic novels. I. Spender, Nik, illustrator II. Title. III. Series: Jeffrey, Gary Graphic medieval history.

DL66.J45 2014 j948'.022 C2014-900367-6
C2014-900368-4

Library of Congress Cataloging-in-Publication Data

Jeffrey, Gary.
The Dark Ages and the Vikings / by Gary Jeffrey ; illustrated by Nick Spender.
pages cm. -- (Graphic medieval history)
Includes index.
ISBN 978-0-7787-0401-0 (reinforced library binding : alk. paper) -- ISBN 978-0-7787-0407-2 (pbk. : alk. paper) -- ISBN 978-1-4271-7513-7 (electronic html) -- ISBN 978-1-4271-7519-9 (electronic pdf)
1. Great Britain--History--Anglo-Saxon period, 449-1066--Juvenile literature. 2. Vikings--Great Britain--Juvenile literature. 3. Great Britain--History--Invasions--Juvenile literature. 4. Great Britain--Civilization--Scandinavian influences--Juvenile literature. 5. Great Britain--History--Norman period, 1066-1154--Juvenile literature. 6. Great Britain--History--Anglo-Saxon period, 449-1066--Comic books, strips, etc. 7. Vikings--Great Britain--Comic books, strips, etc. 8. Graphic novels. I. Spender, Nik, illustrator. II. Title.

DA152.J44 2014
942.01--dc23

2014002263

Contents

After the Romans

The Dark Ages, or early medieval times, began with the collapse of the Roman empire in the 5th century CE. In 285, the Romans had divided their empire in two: the western half would become Europe; the eastern half would become the Byzantine empire. In the west, Germanic tribes formed kingdoms on old Roman lands.

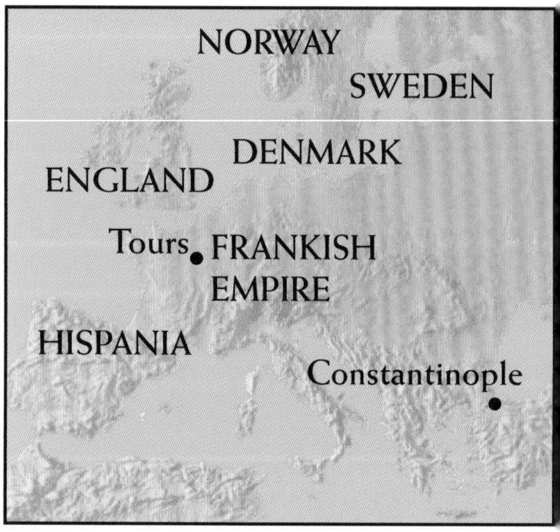
NORWAY
SWEDEN
DENMARK
ENGLAND
Tours
FRANKISH EMPIRE
HISPANIA
Constantinople

Europe during the Dark Ages

The Map of Europe is Drawn

The Germanic tribes included the Angles, Jutes, and Saxons. Their kingdoms set up the borders for much of Europe as we know it today. They traveled from what is now Denmark to Britain, which the Romans had left in 410. Here they created a new people—the Anglo-Saxons, and eventually named their country England.

Another group, the Franks from northern Germany, united all of Gaul (France) under one king and drove the Visigoths (western Goths who had destroyed Rome and formed a kingdom in western France) into Hispania (Spain). The Goths were Germanics from eastern Europe driven west by the Huns—a fierce nomadic tribe. During the 480s, the Ostrogoths (eastern Goths) took over all of Italy.

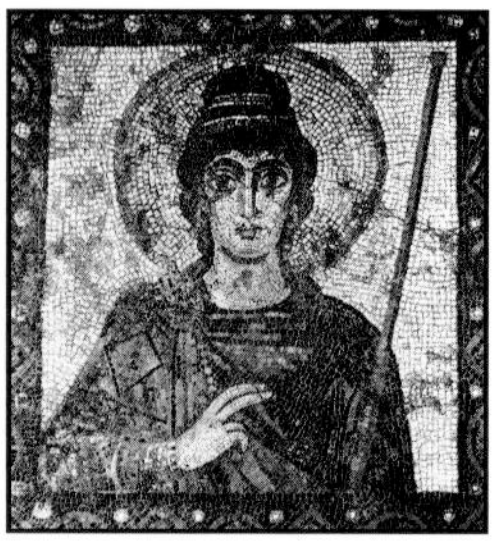

The Byzantines carried on and developed the Roman art of mosaics.

Byzantine Empire

The Byzantine empire in the east was at its most powerful in 555. Its capital was Constantinople (known before as Byzantium, and now as Istanbul, in Turkey). The language and culture they practiced was mainly Greek.

476	481	570	732
Western Roman Empire falls	The Franks are united in France and Germany	Islamic prophet Muhammad is born	The Battle of Tours

Christianity Takes Hold

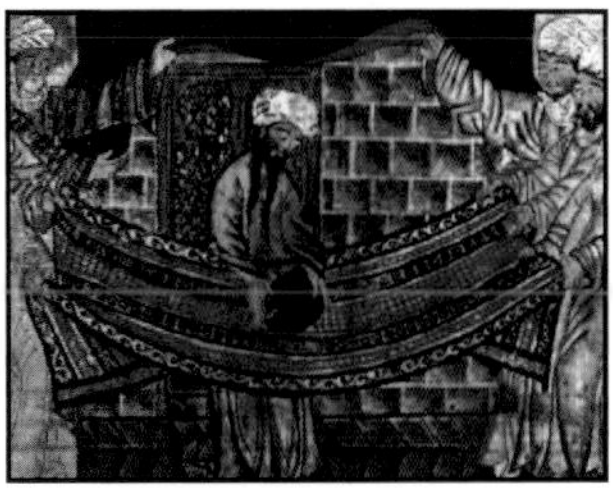

In 570, the prophet Muhammad was born in Mecca, Arabia. He founded the religion of Islam in 622.

Christianity (Roman Catholicism) had been the official religion of the Roman empire since 313. Many of the Germanic tribes had dropped pagan worship to practice their own version of Christianity. The popes of Rome tried to spread Roman Catholicism throughout western Europe. In eastern Europe, they developed their own tradition of Catholic worship.

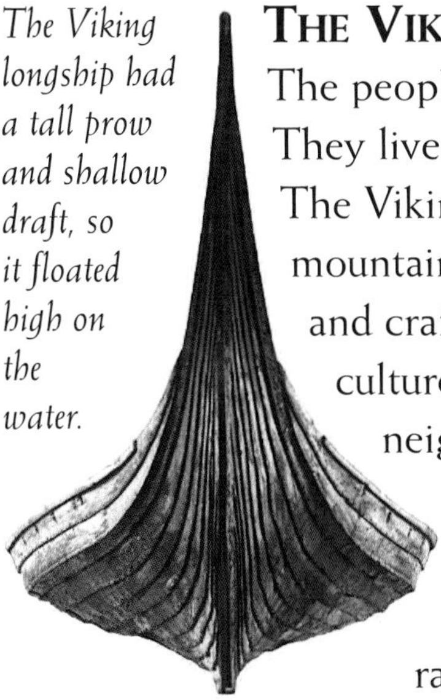

The Viking longship had a tall prow and shallow draft, so it floated high on the water.

The Viking Expansion

The people to the north became known as Vikings. They lived in Norway, Sweden, and northern Denmark. The Vikings lived in coastal communities surrounded by mountainous forests. They were skilled at ship-building and crafts, and traded with other groups. Their warrior culture, however, also glorified raiding their neighbors and fighting battles of honor.

In the 700s, with resources scarce at home, the Vikings set off in their longships in search of trade and plunder. Norwegians raided the north coast of England; Danes raided the south; Swedes sailed deep into the river systems of northeastern Europe. The Norse people were pagan and worshipped many gods including Odin, Thor, and Loki.

Rise of the Moors

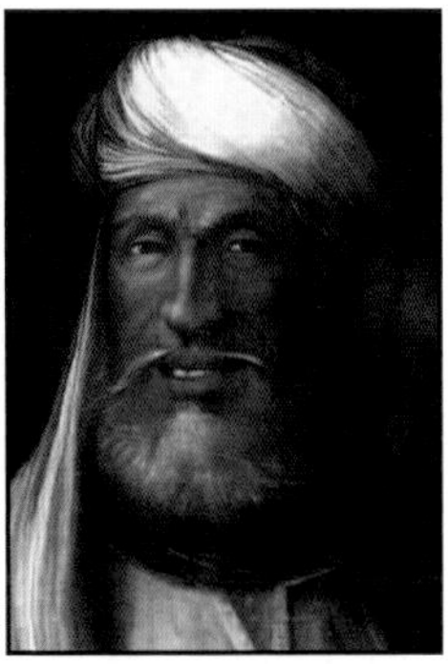

A 17th-century painting of a Moor

The Muslim prophet Muhammad had united Arabia by the time he died in 632. Under a series of leaders of Islamic states, Islam had conquered all of North Africa. Its Muslim people were known as Moors. In 711, the Moors invaded Hispania, conquered the Visigoths, and brought Islam to the edge of Christian Europe.

800	835	896	1066
Charlemagne becomes Holy Roman Emperor	Start of the Viking invasions	Alfred the Great saves England	The Battle of Hastings

Emperors & Kings

In the Battle of Tours in 732, invading Moors were defeated by a Frankish army led by Duke Charles Martel. If Martel had lost, Islam might have become the main religion of Europe.

Charles the Bald, grandson of Duke Charles Martel, became king of the Franks in 786. The Franks' empire grew to cover all of western Europe, and Charles became known as Charlemagne–Charles the Great. In 800, the pope crowned him emperor–the first in 300 years. His empire, called Francia, would one day become the kingdoms of France and Germany.

VIKING INVASIONS

During the 9th century, the Danes stopped raiding and joined forces with the Vikings from Sweden. They formed a large army and landed in England in 865. They were there to conquer. By 871, they had taken East Anglia and York, and threatened Wessex next. Alfred the Great, King of Wessex, paid them to stay away. Mercia was conquered instead, in 874. The following year, the Vikings, led by Guthrum, invaded Wessex again.

Alfred narrowly escaped capture at Chippenham. He reorganized his forces, and in 878, fought and won the final battle to save England from the Vikings.

Viking territory in England was known as the Danelaw. Its capital was Yorvik (York).

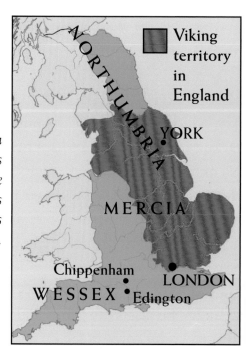

Viking territory in England

NORTHUMBRIA

YORK

MERCIA

Chippenham

WESSEX • Edington

LONDON

ANGLO-SAXON GLORY YEARS

Alfred the Great's grandson, Athelstan, became the first king of the English when the last areas under Viking control finally fell in 927. A succession of kings followed, many ruling for only a short time, until a Danish prince, Canute, invaded in 1016. Canute the Great's 18-year rule was supposedly the greatest in Anglo-Saxon history. The next English king was his stepson, Edward the Confessor, in 1042.

THE NORMANS

Edward had grown up in Normandy, a duchy of France formed in 911. Normans, meaning Northmen, were descendants of the Vikings and Franks. They had developed a highly organized warrior culture and fought against other duchies. They were also skilled hunters, horsemen, and builders.

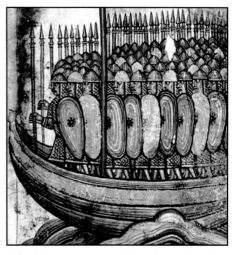

The Normans were short-haired and clean-shaven. Although not great seafarers, they traveled in Viking-style boats. Their warriors wore chain mail shirts.

DOUBTFUL SUCCESSION

Edward the Confessor ruled England with Godwin, Earl of Wessex, as his powerful right-hand man. In 1051, Godwin fell out of favor with the king and was exiled. But when Godwin died, his son, Harold, became Edward's aide.

While Harold II waited on the Isle of Wight for the Norman invasion, another fight for his throne was brewing in Denmark.

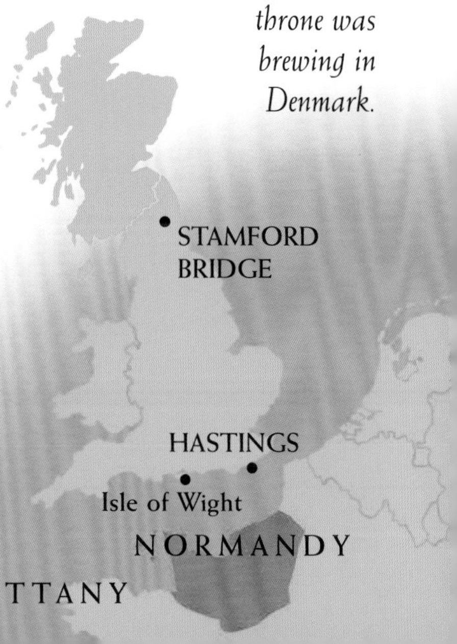

By 1065, Edward was aging and childless. Harold Godwinson became shipwrecked and came under the care of William, the young Duke of Normandy. William asked Harold for his help in gaining the throne of England. He claimed Edward had promised it to him when he visited the king when Godwin was in exile.

But when Edward died in 1066, the Anglo-Saxon Witan, or council of elders, crowned Harold king instead. The news made William so angry he raised an army and vowed to take the crown by force.

STAMFORD BRIDGE

HASTINGS

Isle of Wight

NORMANDY

BRITTANY

The Raid on Lindisfarne

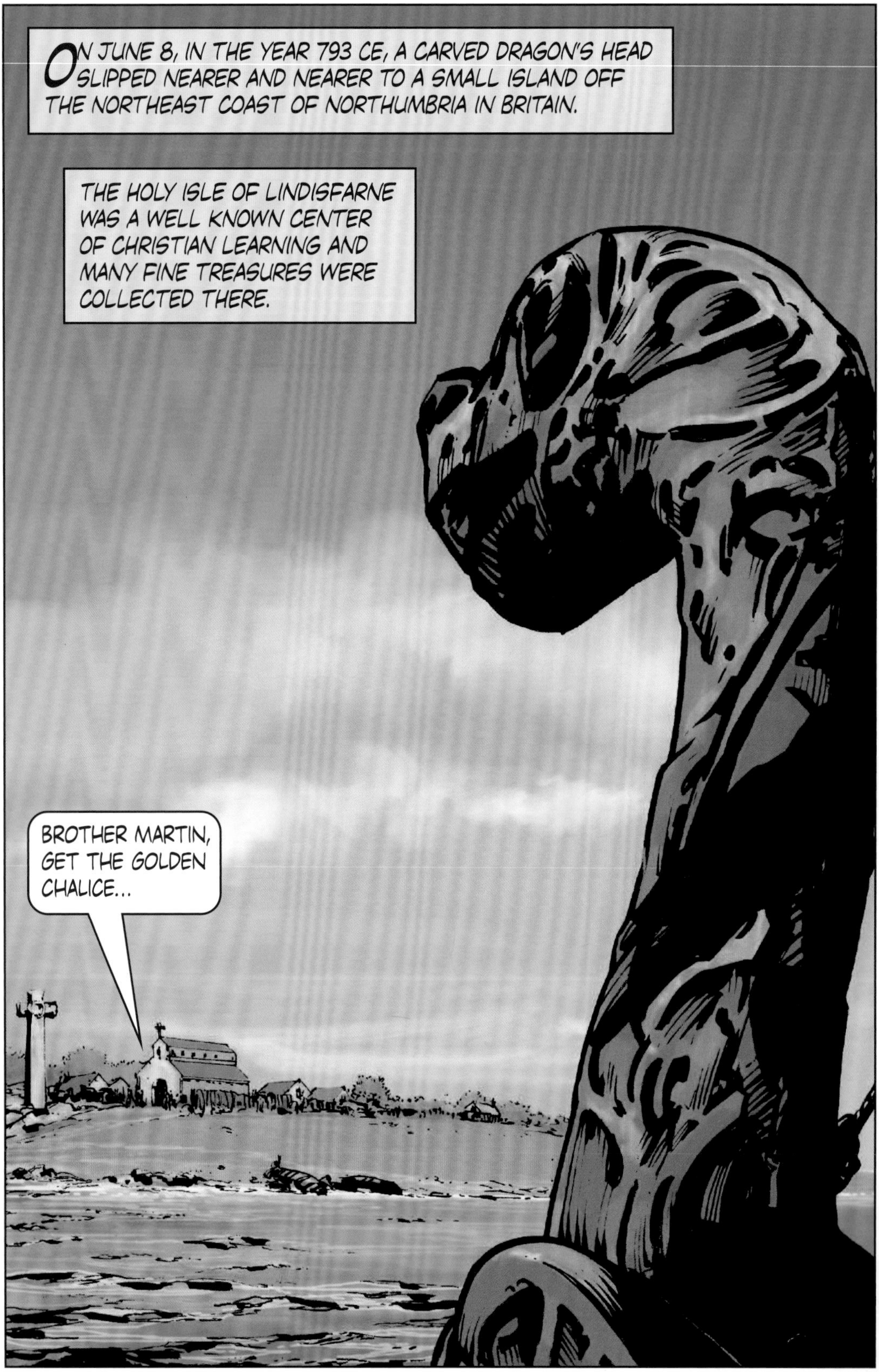
ON JUNE 8, IN THE YEAR 793 CE, A CARVED DRAGON'S HEAD SLIPPED NEARER AND NEARER TO A SMALL ISLAND OFF THE NORTHEAST COAST OF NORTHUMBRIA IN BRITAIN.
THE HOLY ISLE OF LINDISFARNE WAS A WELL KNOWN CENTER OF CHRISTIAN LEARNING AND MANY FINE TREASURES WERE COLLECTED THERE.
BROTHER MARTIN, GET THE GOLDEN CHALICE...

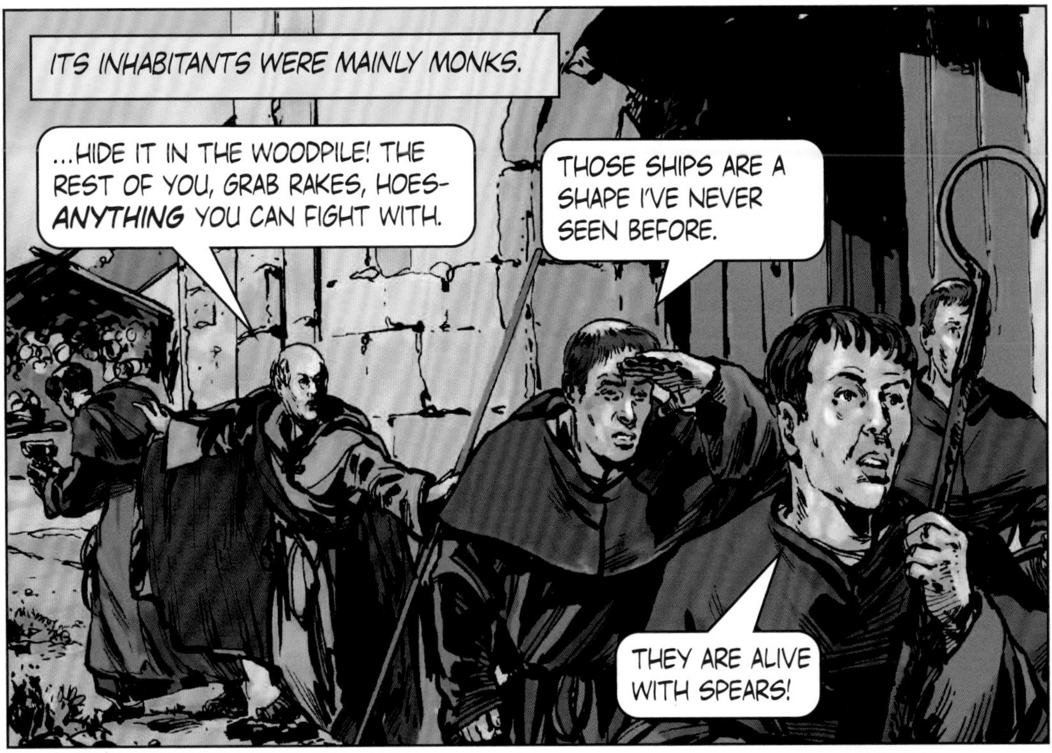
ITS INHABITANTS WERE MAINLY MONKS.
...HIDE IT IN THE WOODPILE! THE REST OF YOU, GRAB RAKES, HOES- ANYTHING YOU CAN FIGHT WITH.
THOSE SHIPS ARE A SHAPE I'VE NEVER SEEN BEFORE.
THEY ARE ALIVE WITH SPEARS!

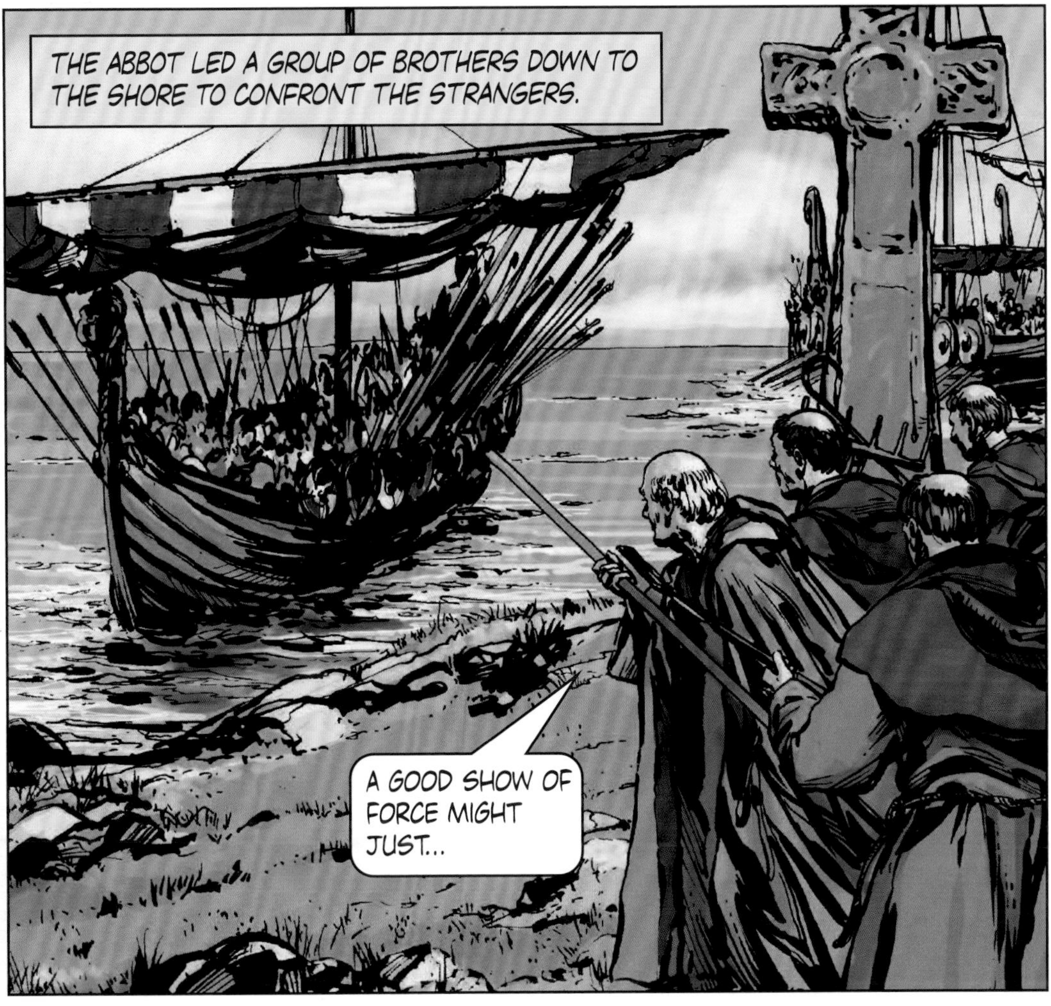
THE ABBOT LED A GROUP OF BROTHERS DOWN TO THE SHORE TO CONFRONT THE STRANGERS.
A GOOD SHOW OF FORCE MIGHT JUST...

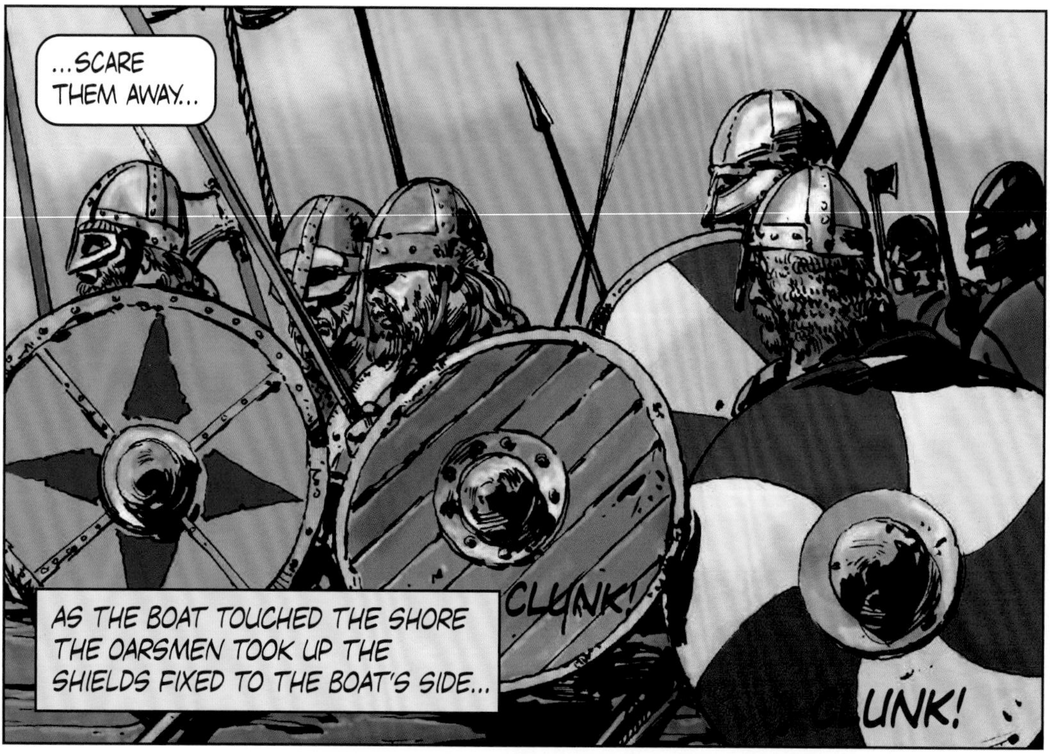
...SCARE THEM AWAY...
AS THE BOAT TOUCHED THE SHORE THE OARSMEN TOOK UP THE SHIELDS FIXED TO THE BOAT'S SIDE...
CLUNK!
UNK!

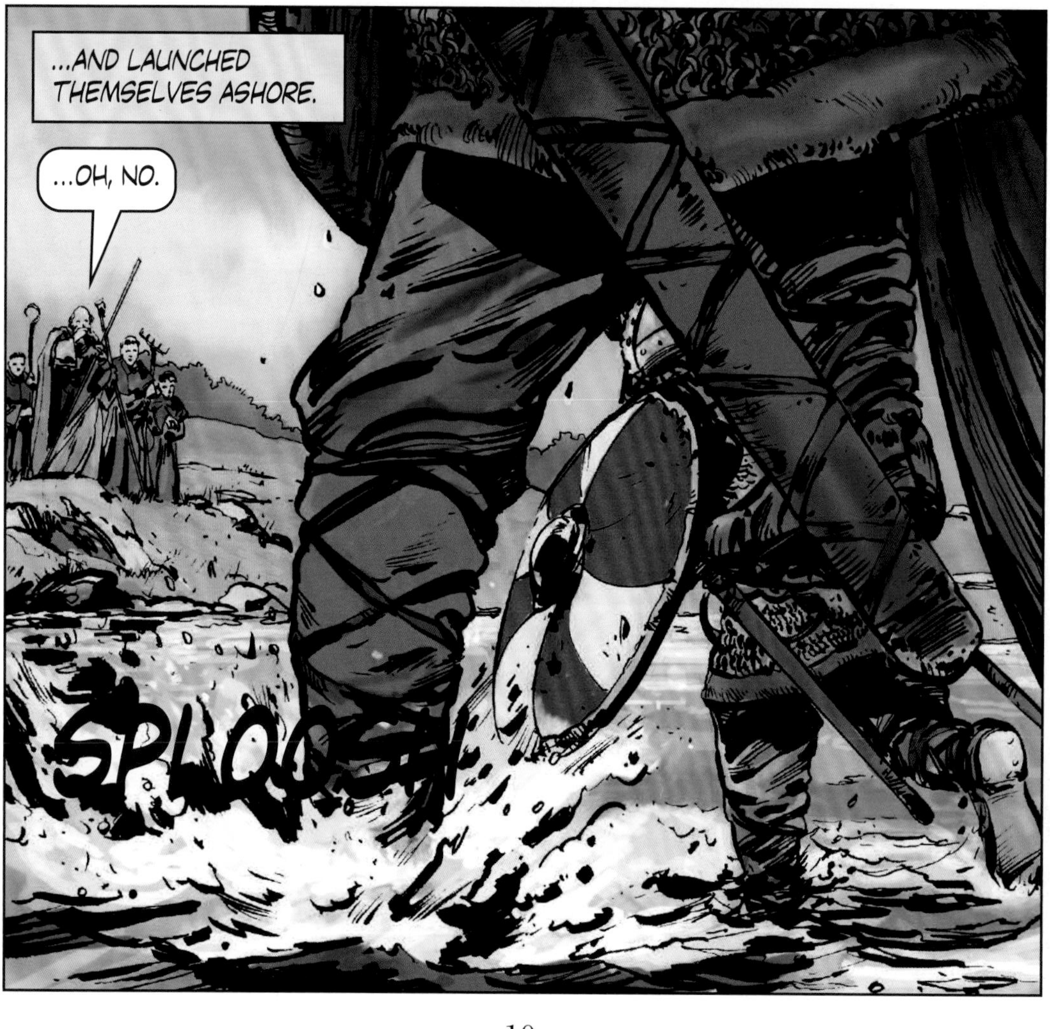
...AND LAUNCHED THEMSELVES ASHORE.
...OH, NO.
SPLOOSH

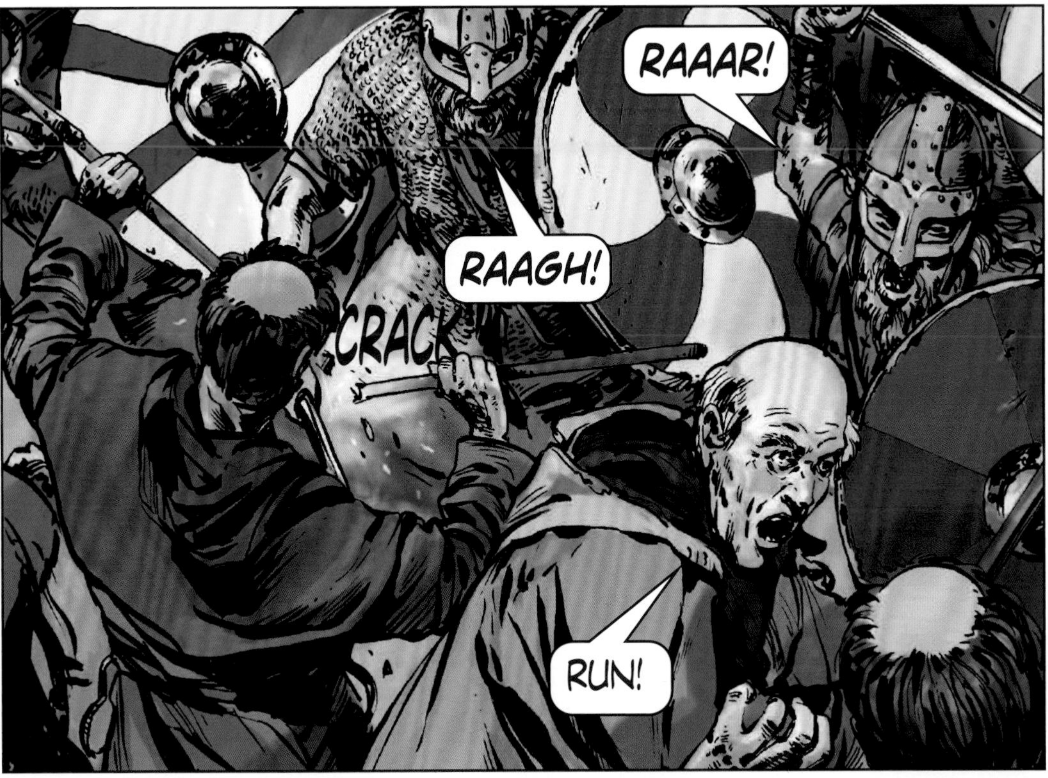
RAAAR!
RAAGH!
CRACK
RUN!

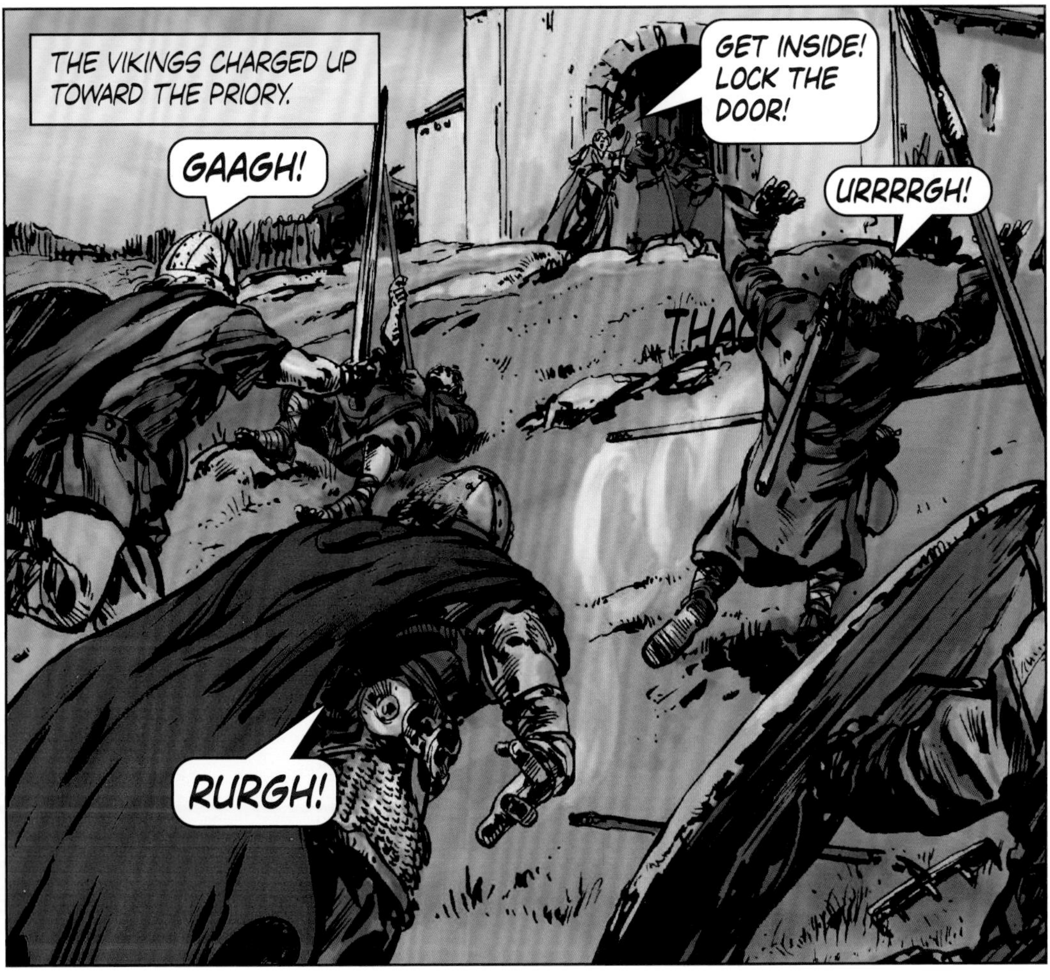
THE VIKINGS CHARGED UP TOWARD THE PRIORY.
GET INSIDE! LOCK THE DOOR!
GAAGH!
URRRRGH!
RURGH!

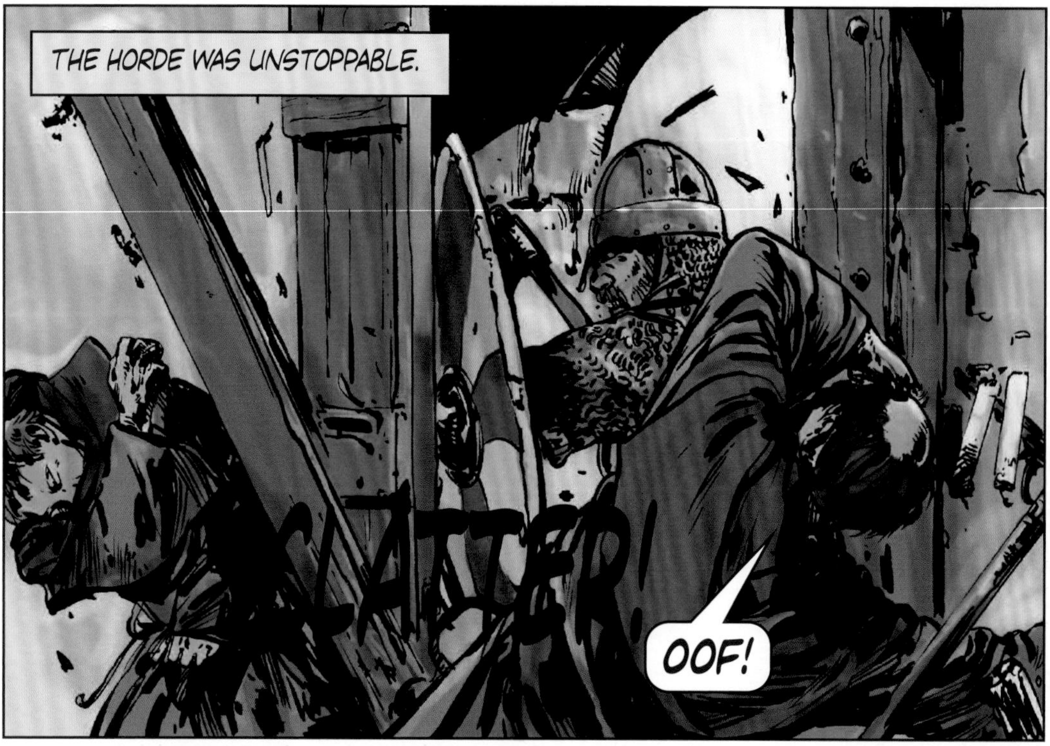
THE HORDE WAS UNSTOPPABLE.
CLATTER!
OOF!

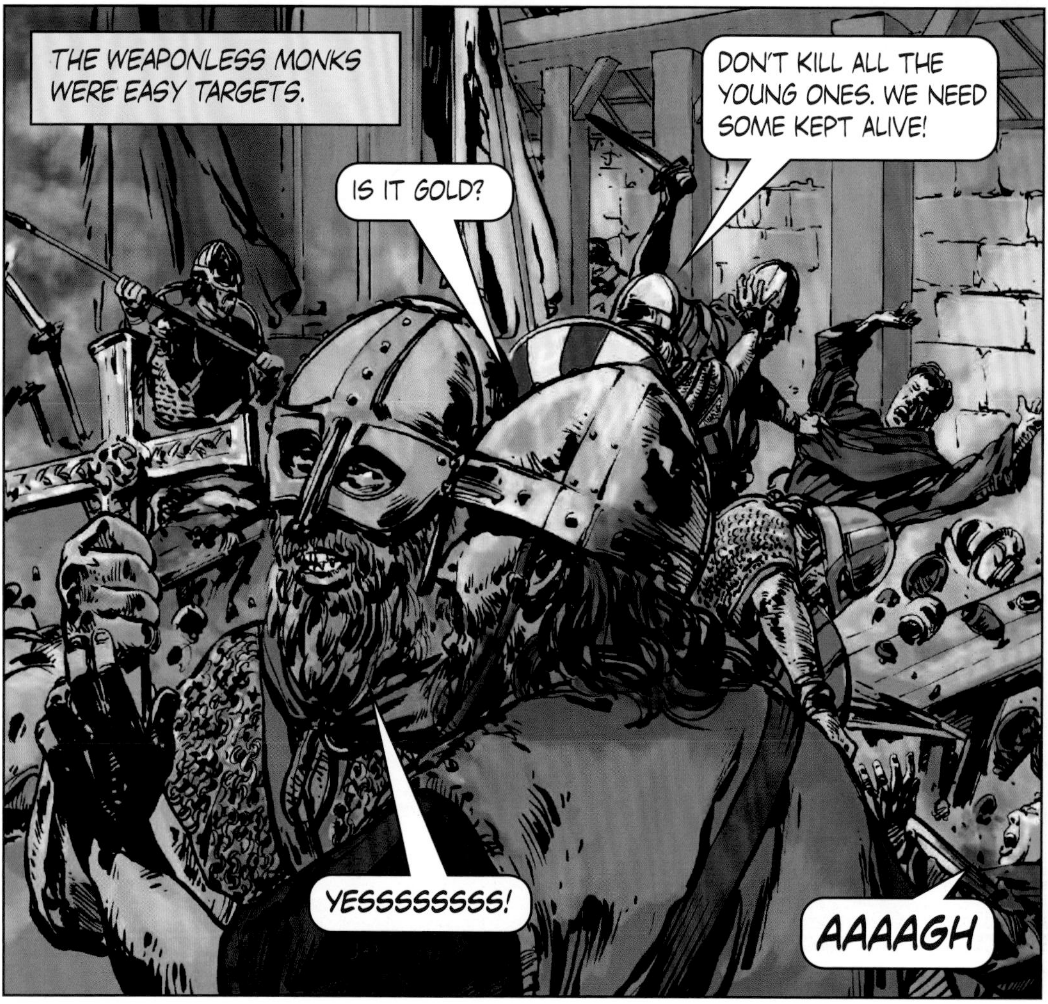
THE WEAPONLESS MONKS WERE EASY TARGETS.
DON'T KILL ALL THE YOUNG ONES. WE NEED SOME KEPT ALIVE!
IS IT GOLD?
YESSSSSSSS!
AAAAGH

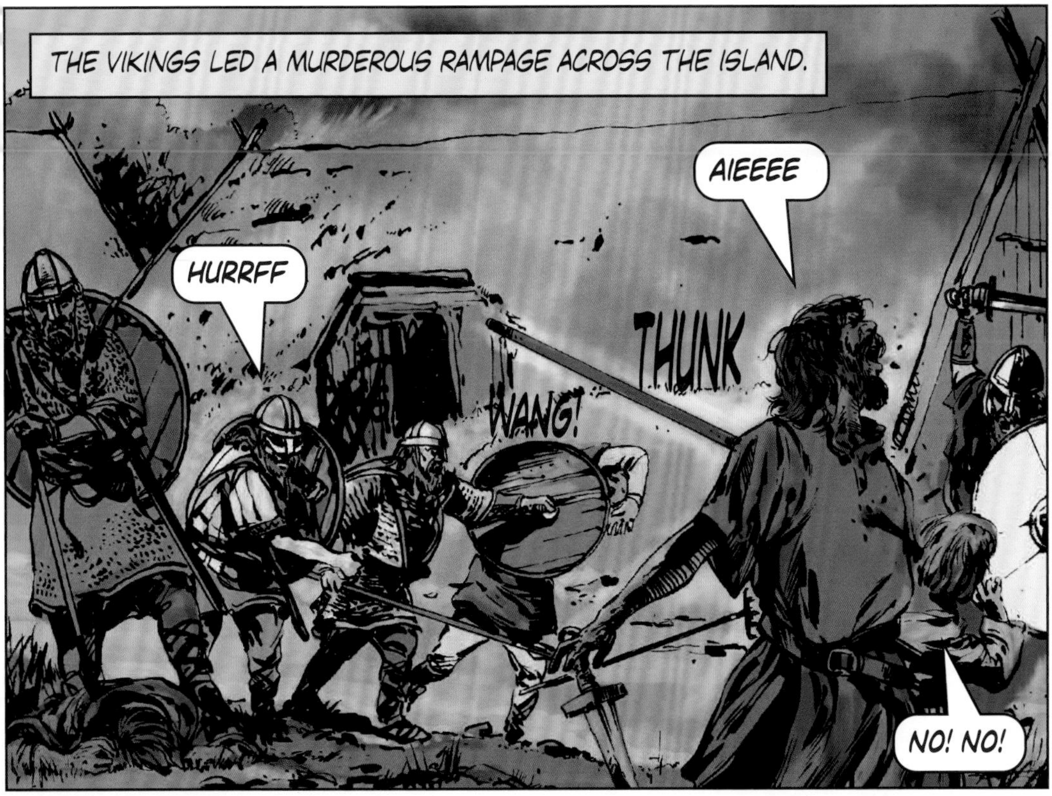
THE VIKINGS LED A MURDEROUS RAMPAGE ACROSS THE ISLAND.
HURRFF
WANG!
THUNK
AIEEEE
NO! NO!

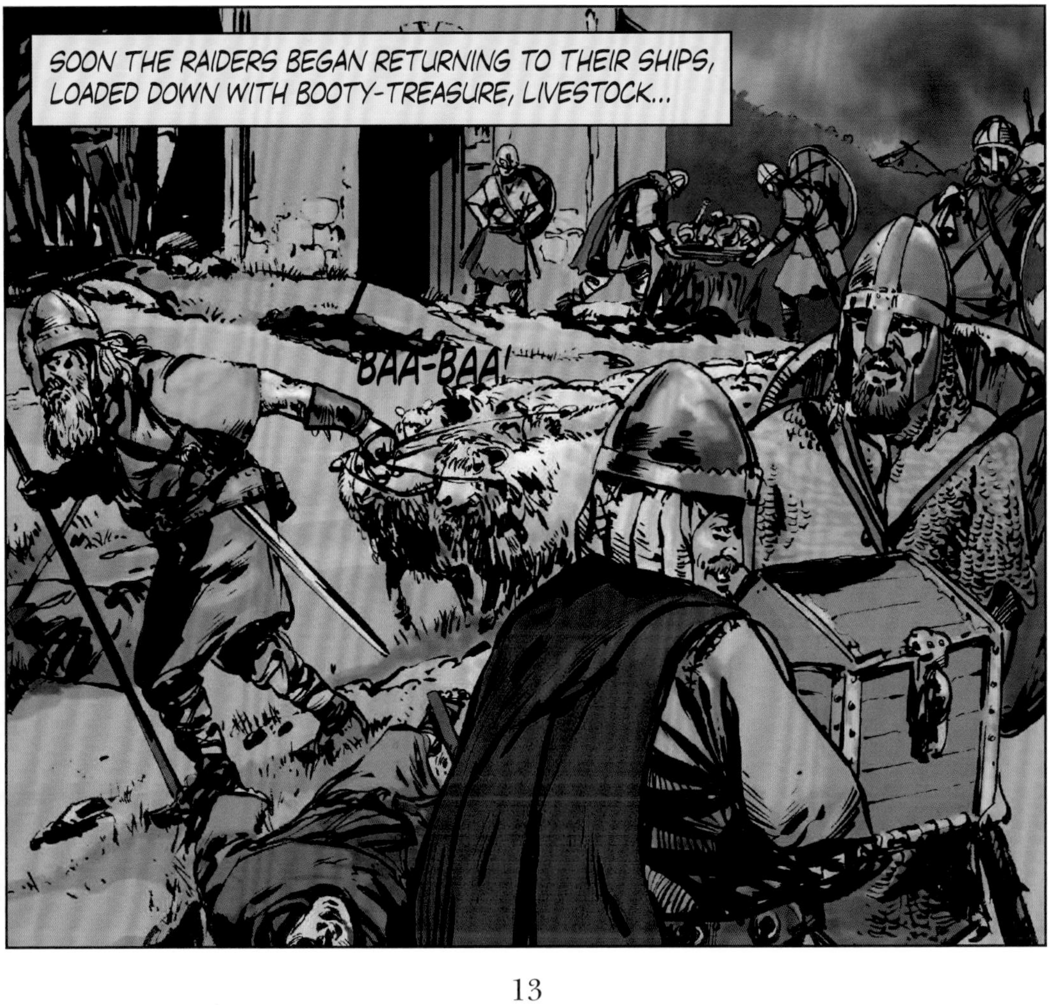
SOON THE RAIDERS BEGAN RETURNING TO THEIR SHIPS, LOADED DOWN WITH BOOTY-TREASURE, LIVESTOCK...
BAA-BAA!

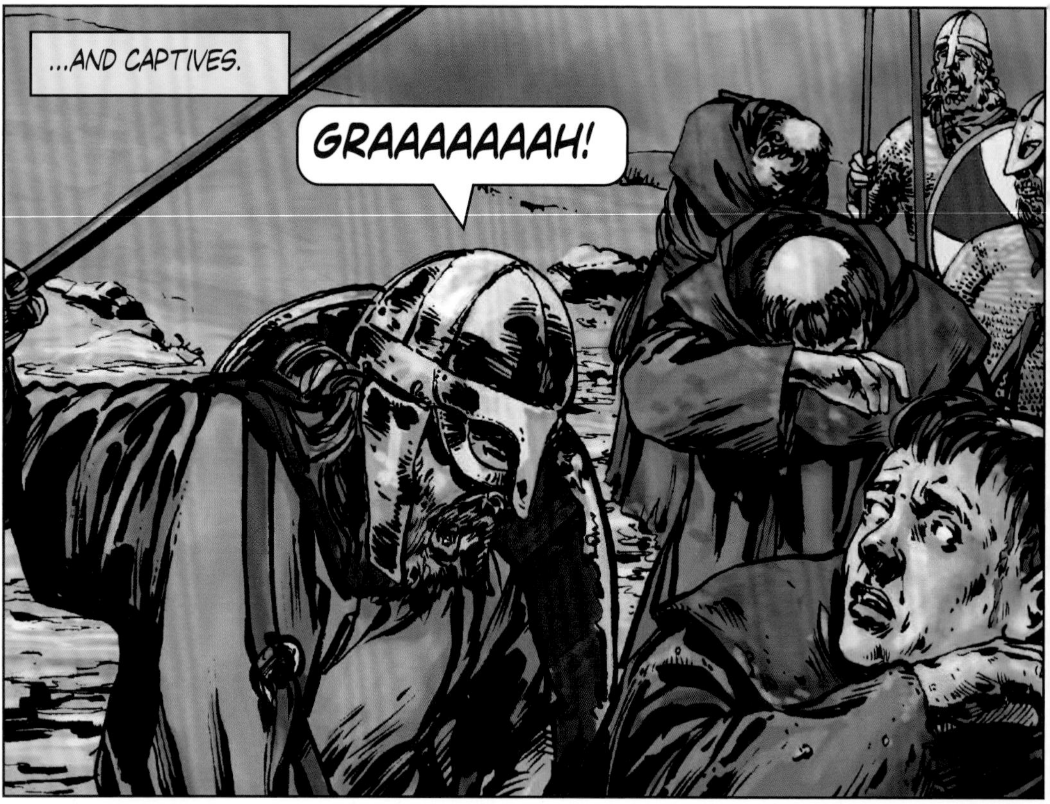
...AND CAPTIVES.
GRAAAAAAAH!

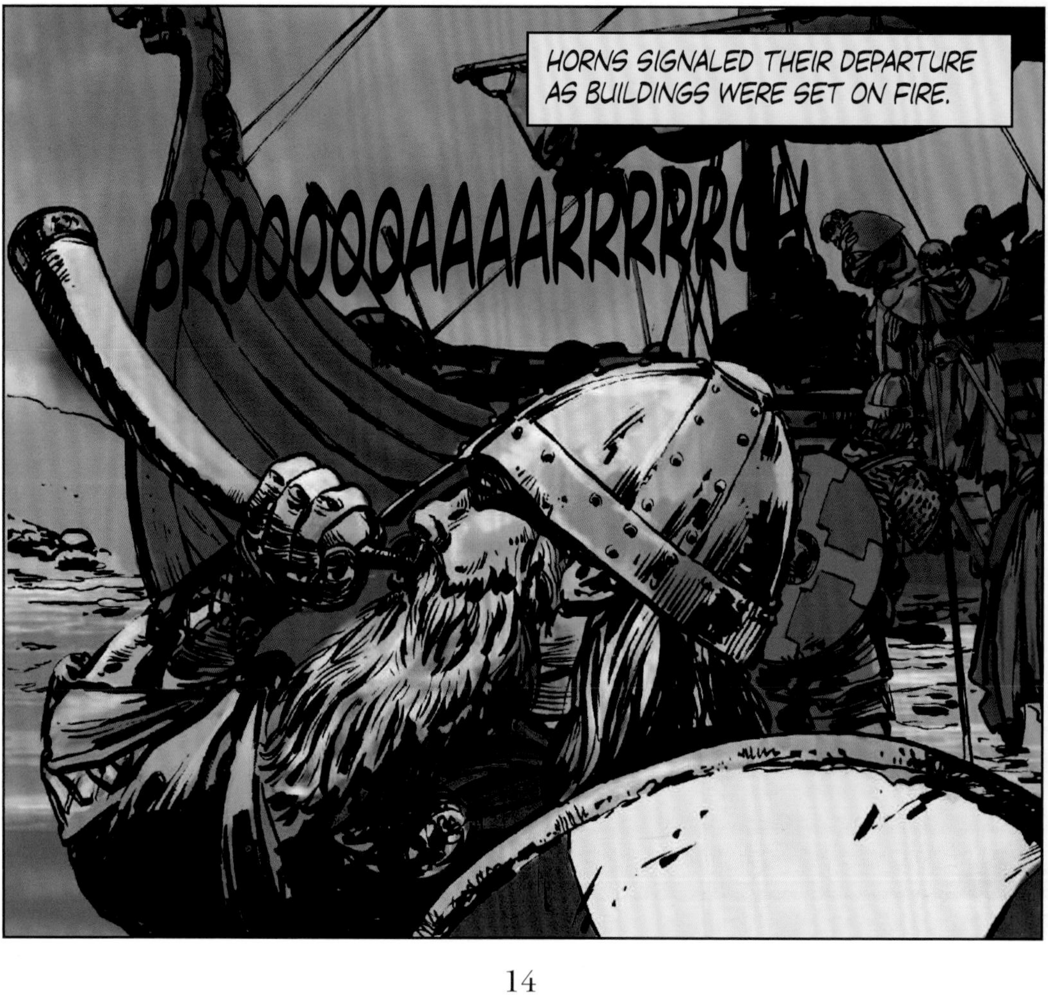
HORNS SIGNALED THEIR DEPARTURE AS BUILDINGS WERE SET ON FIRE.
BROOOOOAAAARRRRROA

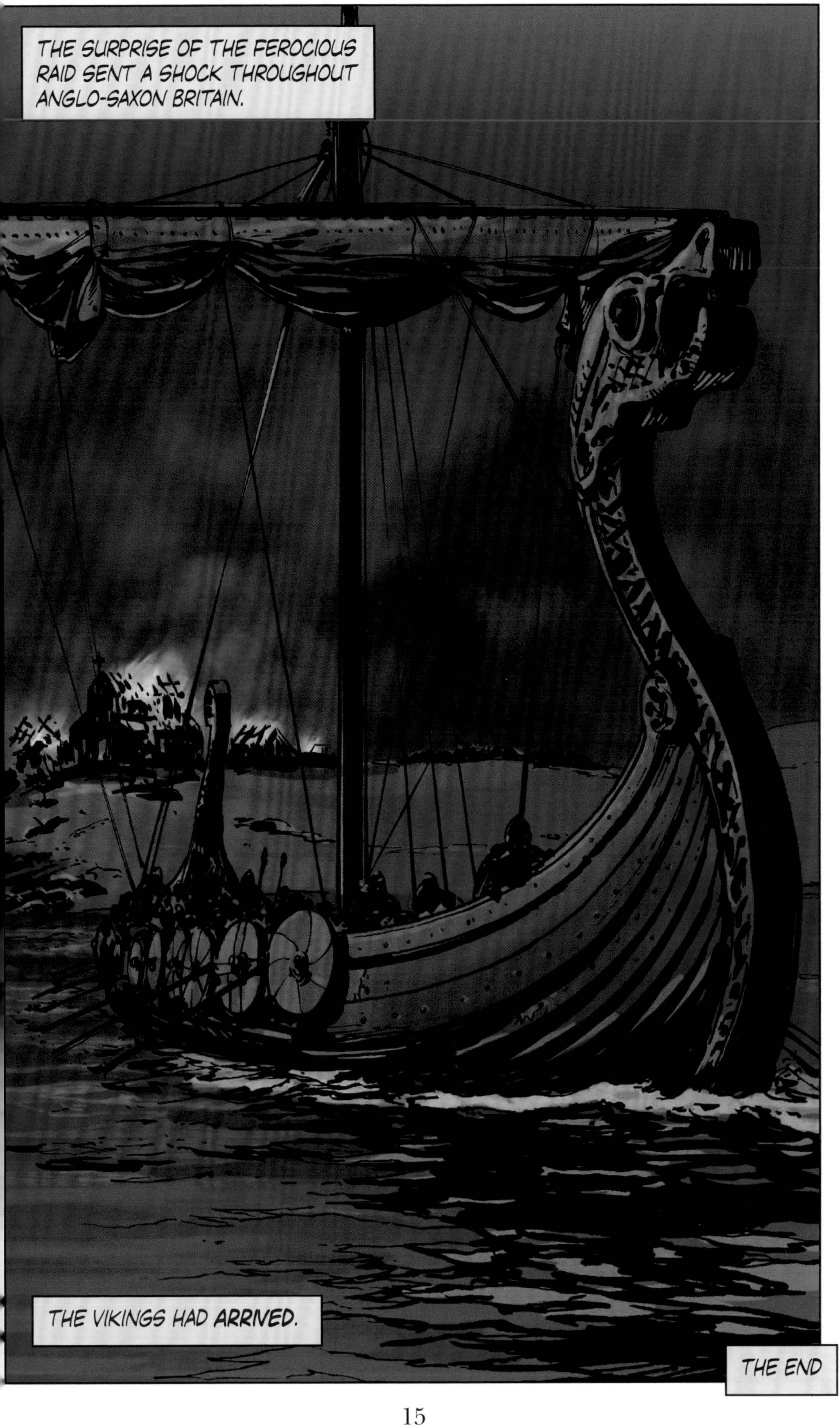
THE SURPRISE OF THE FEROCIOUS RAID SENT A SHOCK THROUGHOUT ANGLO-SAXON BRITAIN.
THE VIKINGS HAD ARRIVED.
THE END

The Battle of Edington

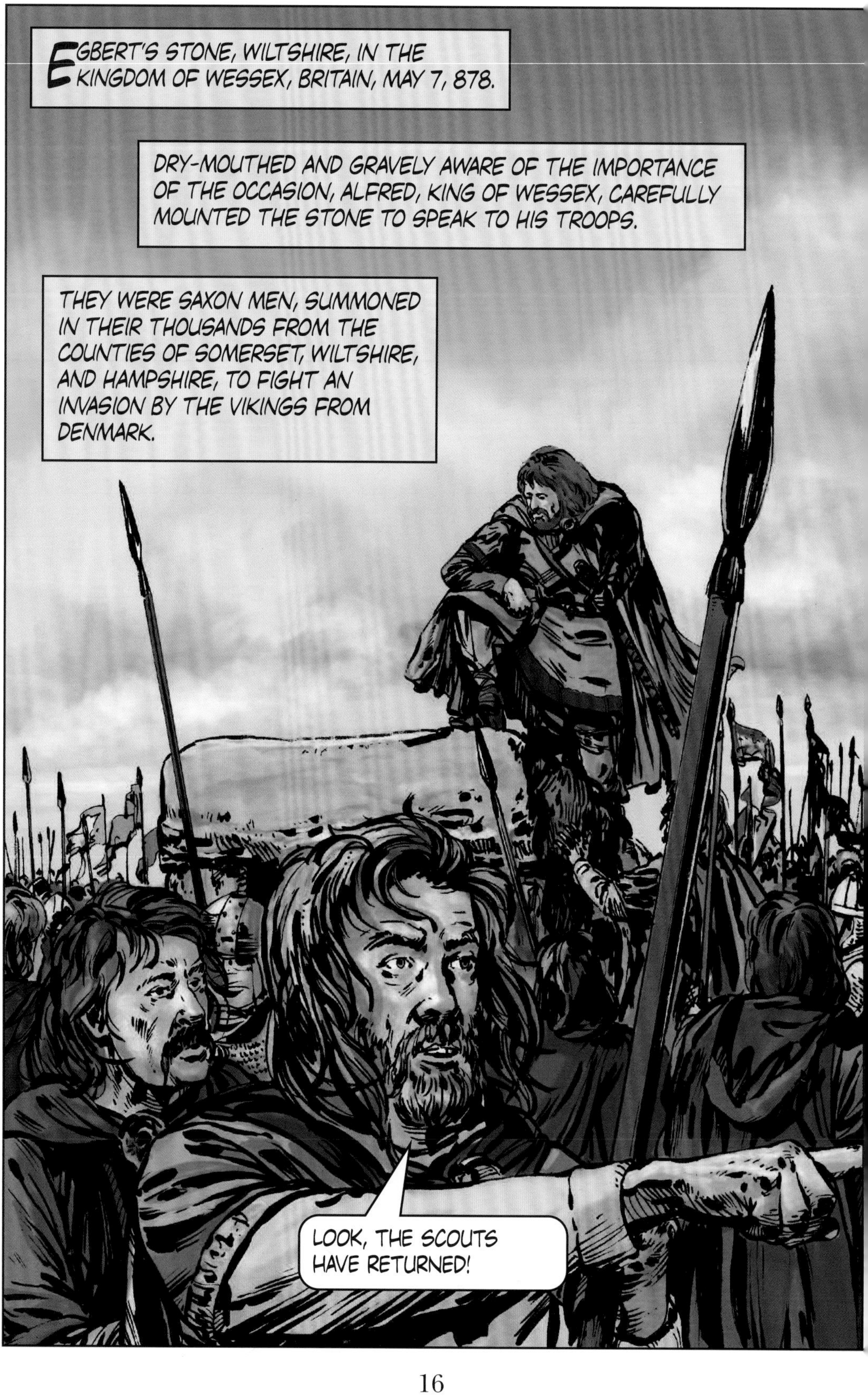
EGBERT'S STONE, WILTSHIRE, IN THE KINGDOM OF WESSEX, BRITAIN, MAY 7, 878.
DRY-MOUTHED AND GRAVELY AWARE OF THE IMPORTANCE OF THE OCCASION, ALFRED, KING OF WESSEX, CAREFULLY MOUNTED THE STONE TO SPEAK TO HIS TROOPS.
THEY WERE SAXON MEN, SUMMONED IN THEIR THOUSANDS FROM THE COUNTIES OF SOMERSET, WILTSHIRE, AND HAMPSHIRE, TO FIGHT AN INVASION BY THE VIKINGS FROM DENMARK.
LOOK, THE SCOUTS HAVE RETURNED!

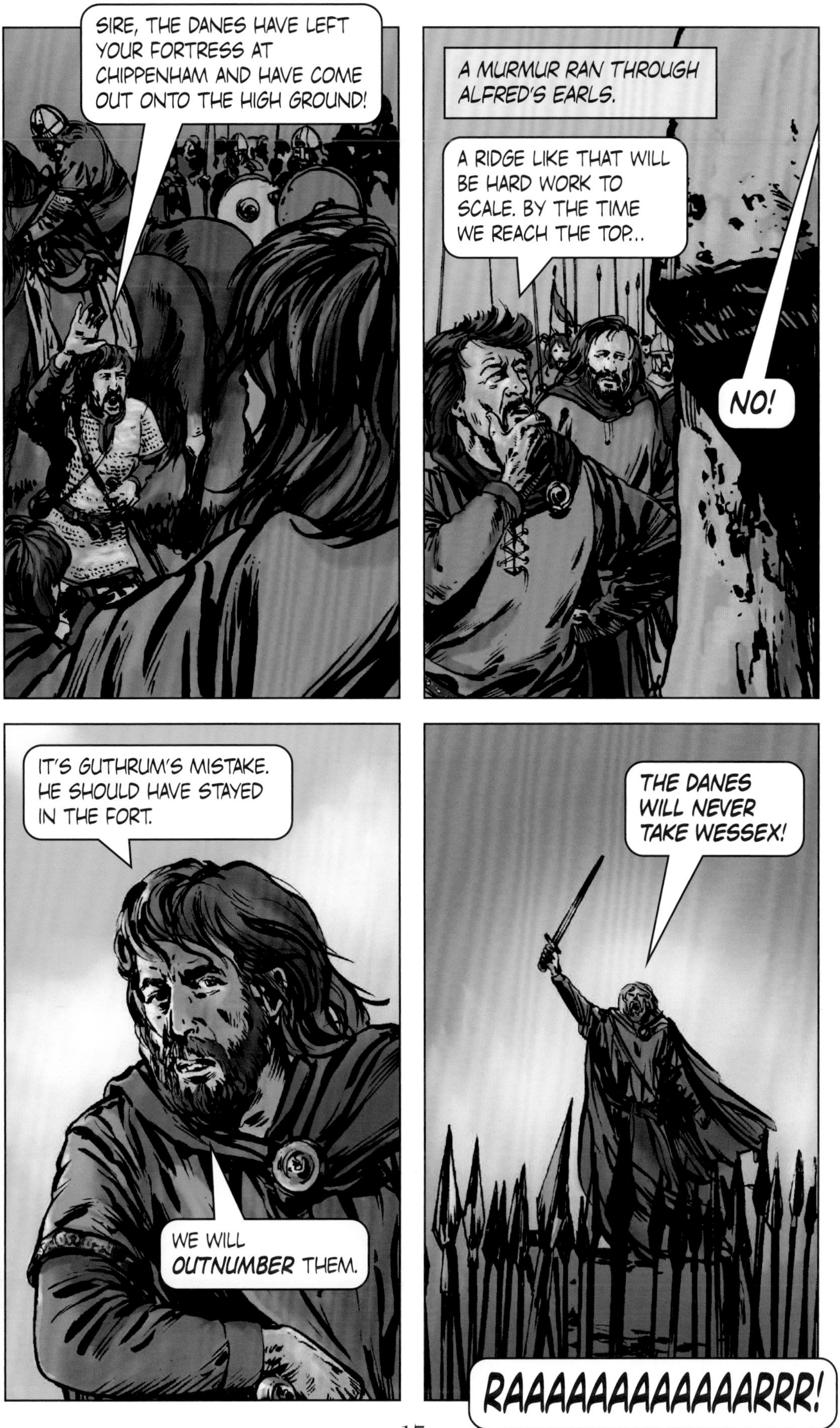
SIRE, THE DANES HAVE LEFT YOUR FORTRESS AT CHIPPENHAM AND HAVE COME OUT ONTO THE HIGH GROUND!
A MURMUR RAN THROUGH ALFRED'S EARLS.
A RIDGE LIKE THAT WILL BE HARD WORK TO SCALE. BY THE TIME WE REACH THE TOP...
NO!
IT'S GUTHRUM'S MISTAKE. HE SHOULD HAVE STAYED IN THE FORT.
WE WILL OUTNUMBER THEM.
THE DANES WILL NEVER TAKE WESSEX!
RAAAAAAAAAAAARRR!

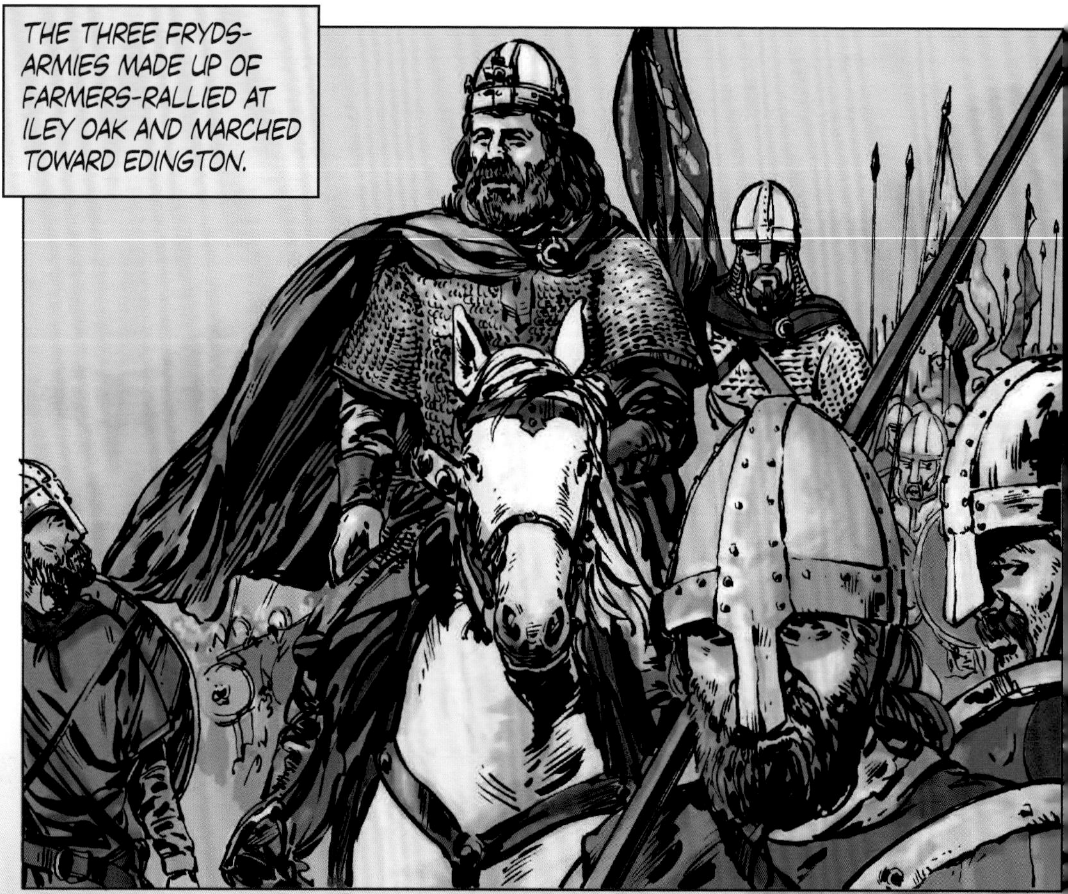
THE THREE FRYDS-ARMIES MADE UP OF FARMERS-RALLIED AT ILEY OAK AND MARCHED TOWARD EDINGTON.

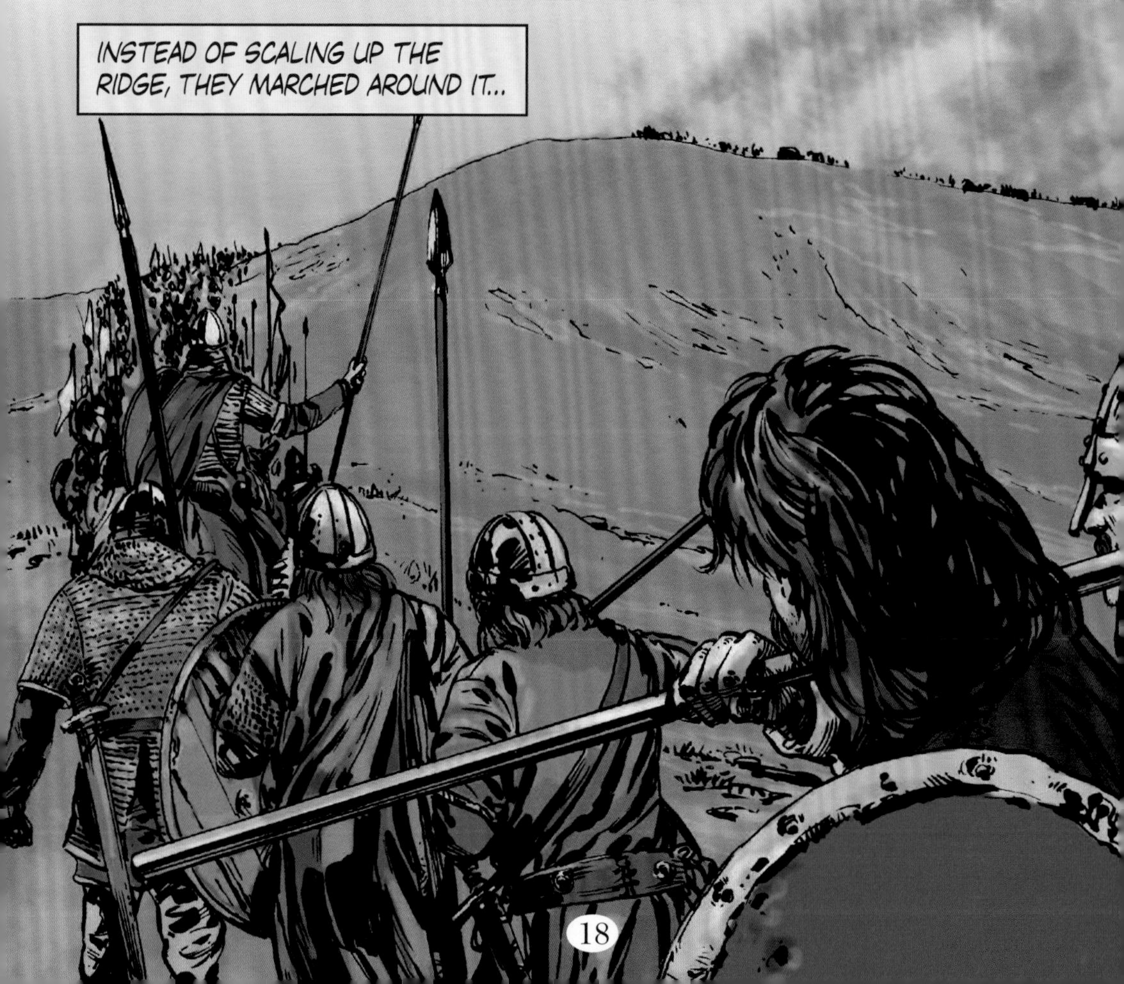
INSTEAD OF SCALING UP THE RIDGE, THEY MARCHED AROUND IT...

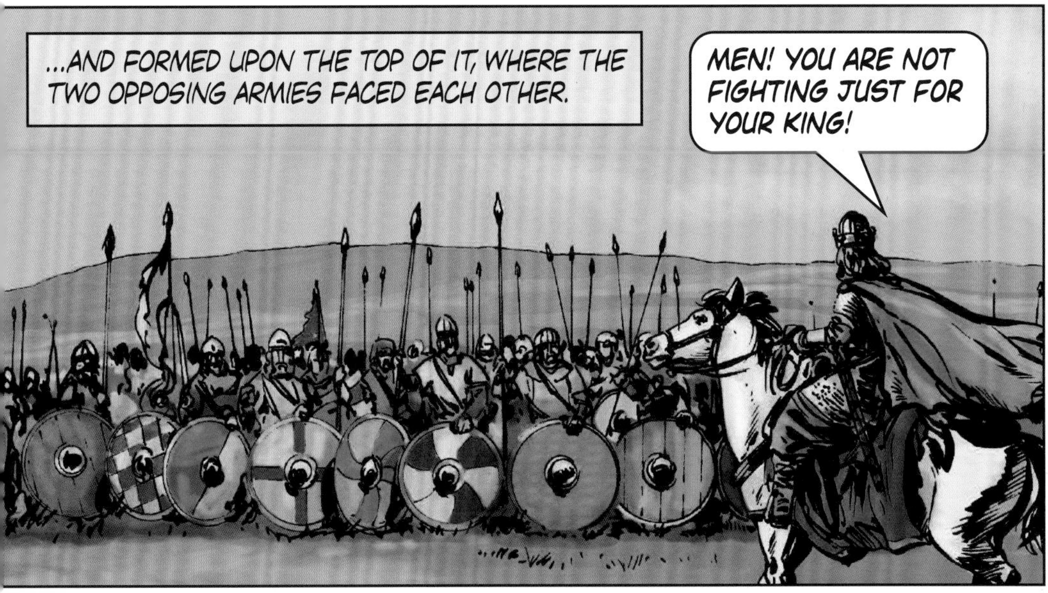
...AND FORMED UPON THE TOP OF IT, WHERE THE TWO OPPOSING ARMIES FACED EACH OTHER.
MEN! YOU ARE NOT FIGHTING JUST FOR YOUR KING!

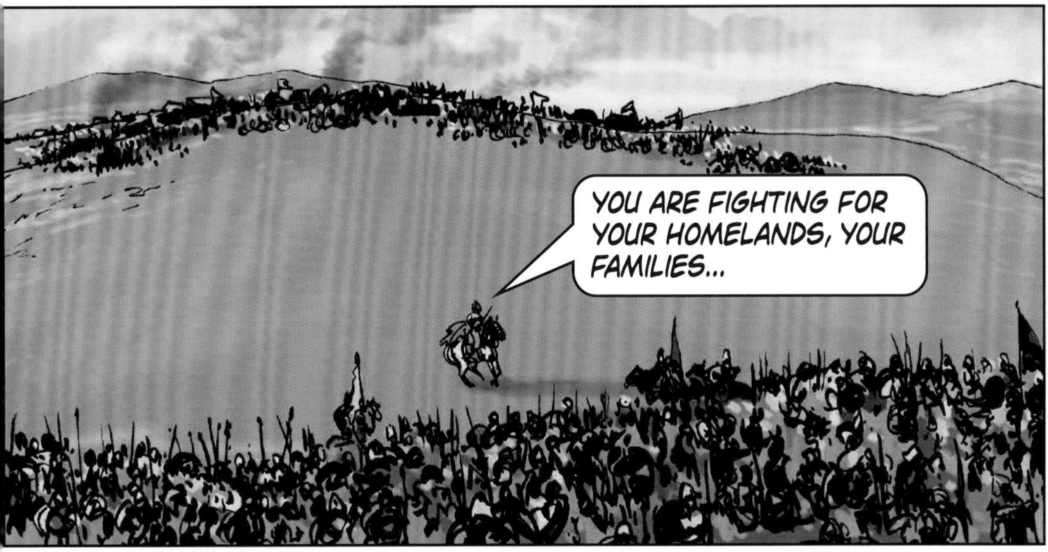
YOU ARE FIGHTING FOR YOUR HOMELANDS, YOUR FAMILIES...

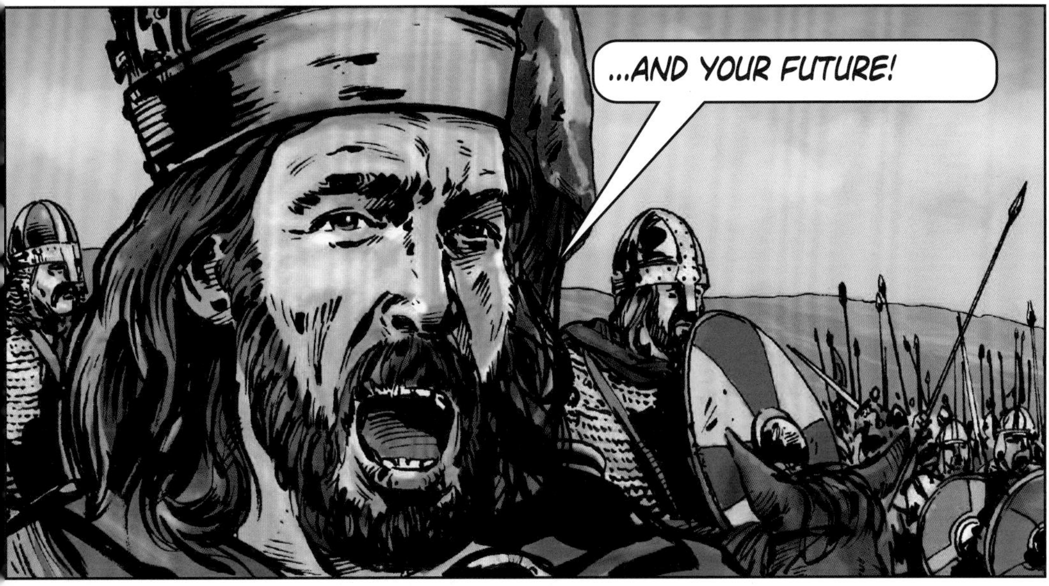
...AND YOUR FUTURE!

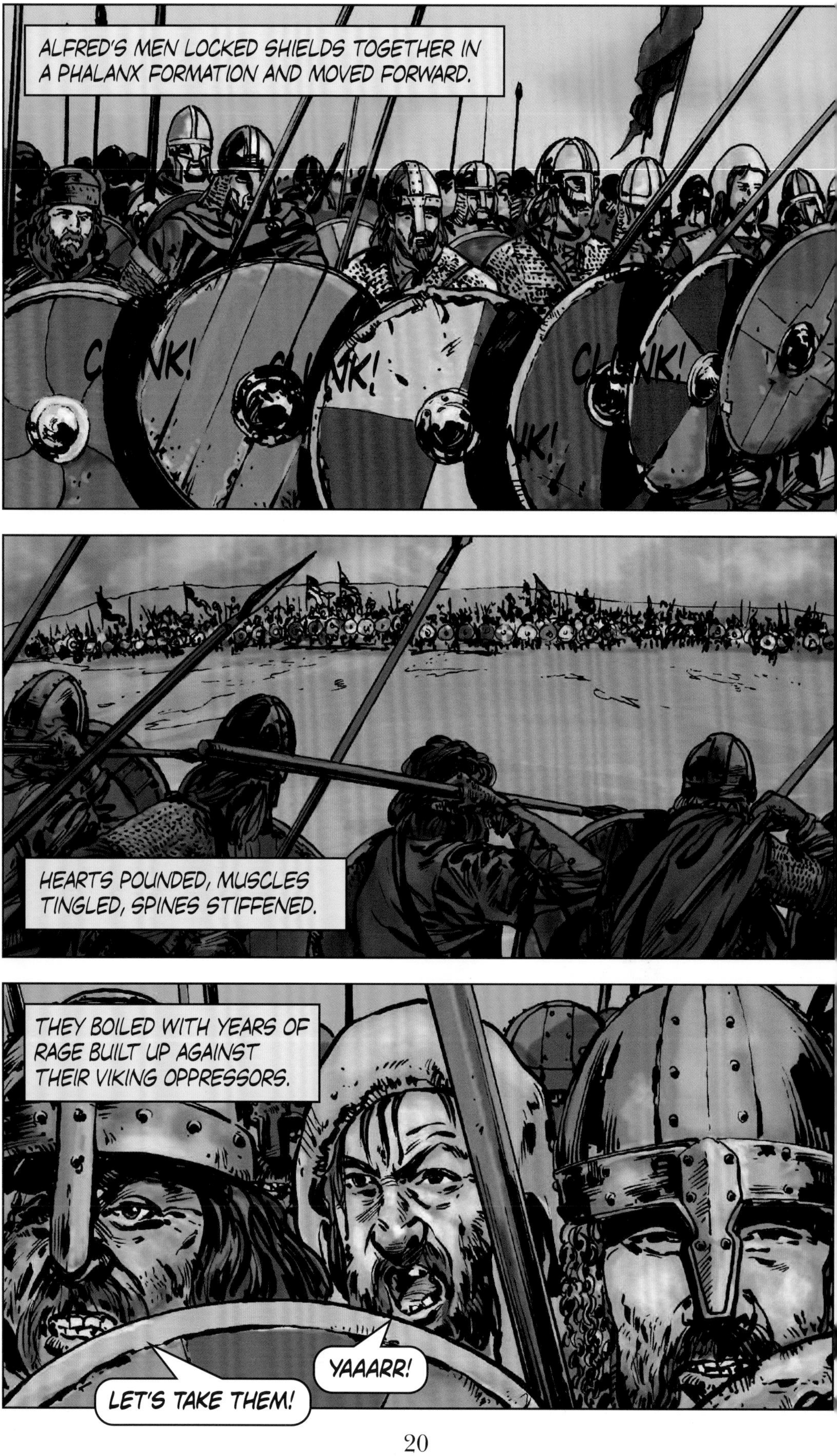
ALFRED'S MEN LOCKED SHIELDS TOGETHER IN A PHALANX FORMATION AND MOVED FORWARD.
HEARTS POUNDED, MUSCLES TINGLED, SPINES STIFFENED.
THEY BOILED WITH YEARS OF RAGE BUILT UP AGAINST THEIR VIKING OPPRESSORS.
YAAARR!
LET'S TAKE THEM!

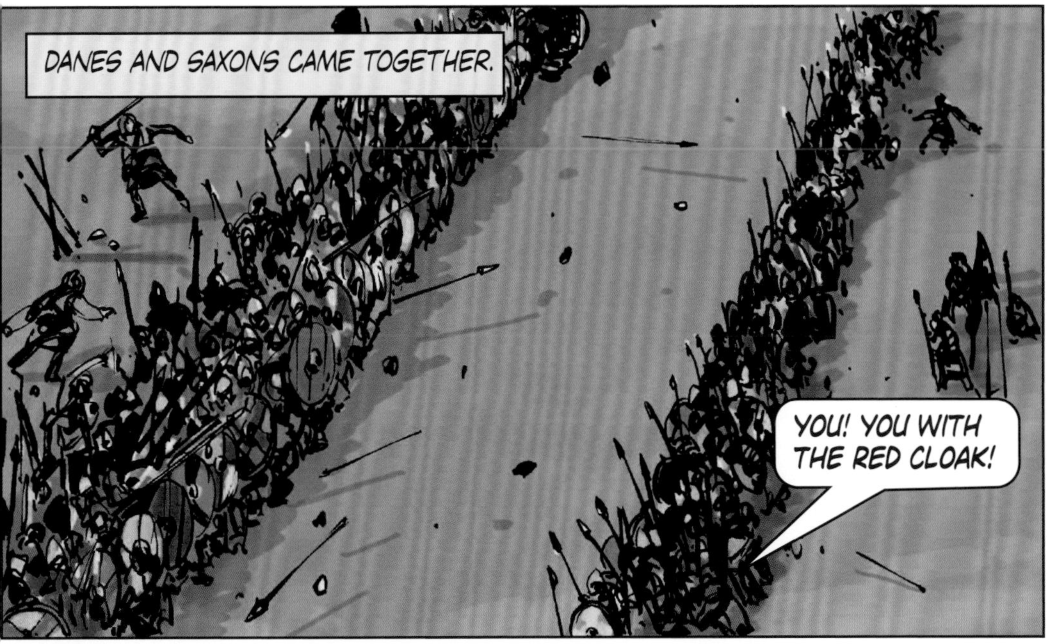
DANES AND SAXONS CAME TOGETHER.
YOU! YOU WITH THE RED CLOAK!

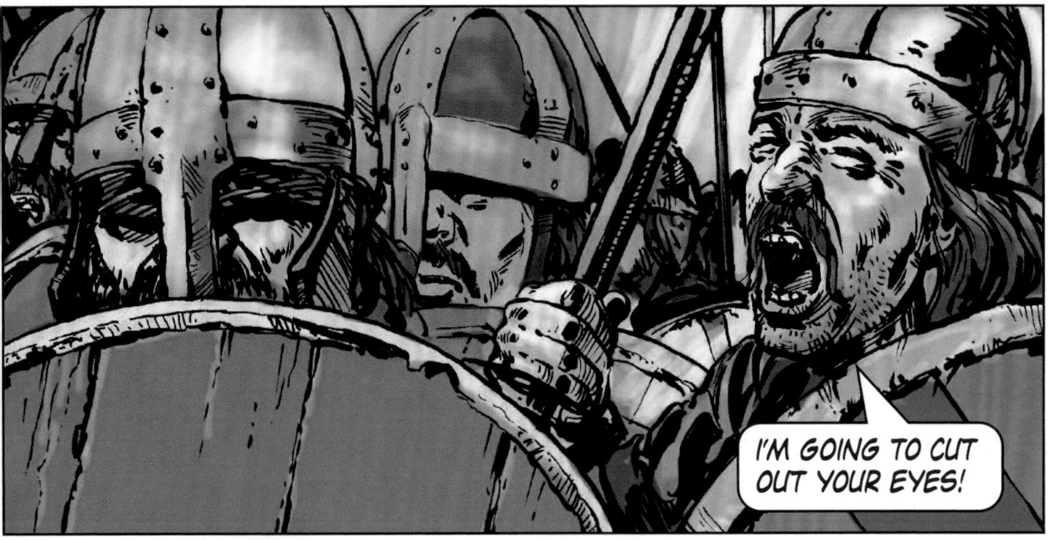
I'M GOING TO CUT OUT YOUR EYES!

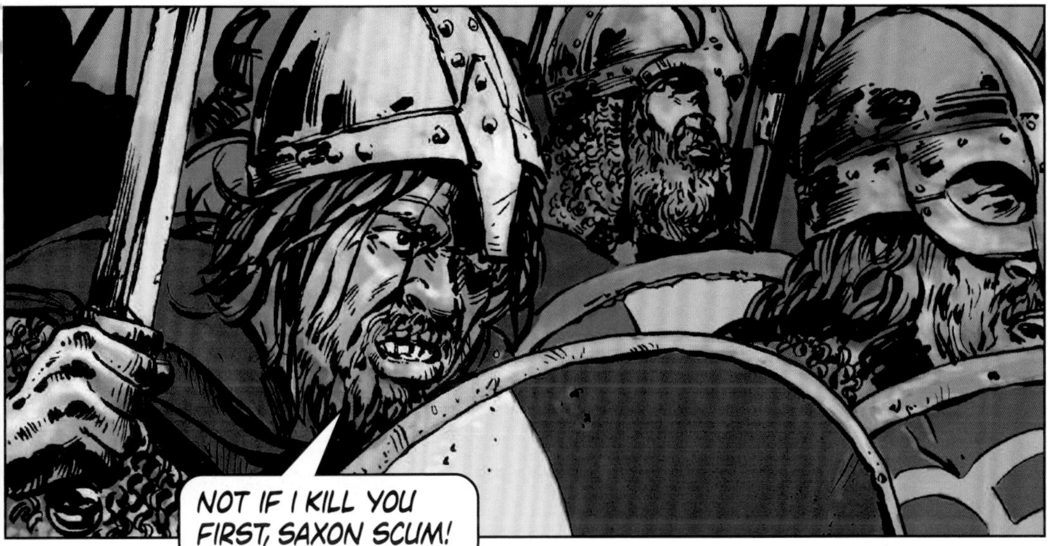
NOT IF I KILL YOU FIRST, SAXON SCUM!

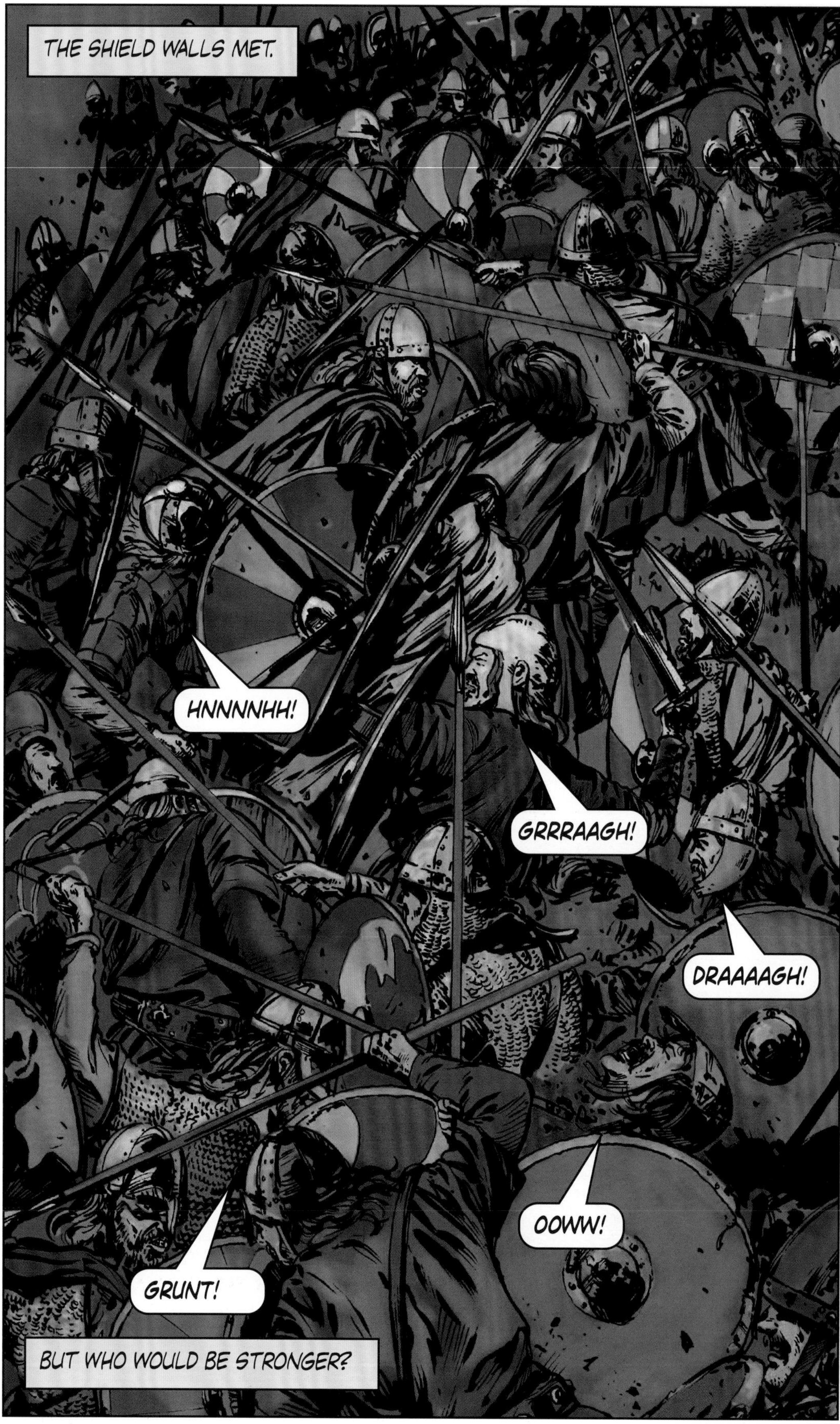
THE SHIELD WALLS MET.
HNNNNHH!
GRRRAAGH!
DRAAAAGH!
OOWW!
GRUNT!
BUT WHO WOULD BE STRONGER?

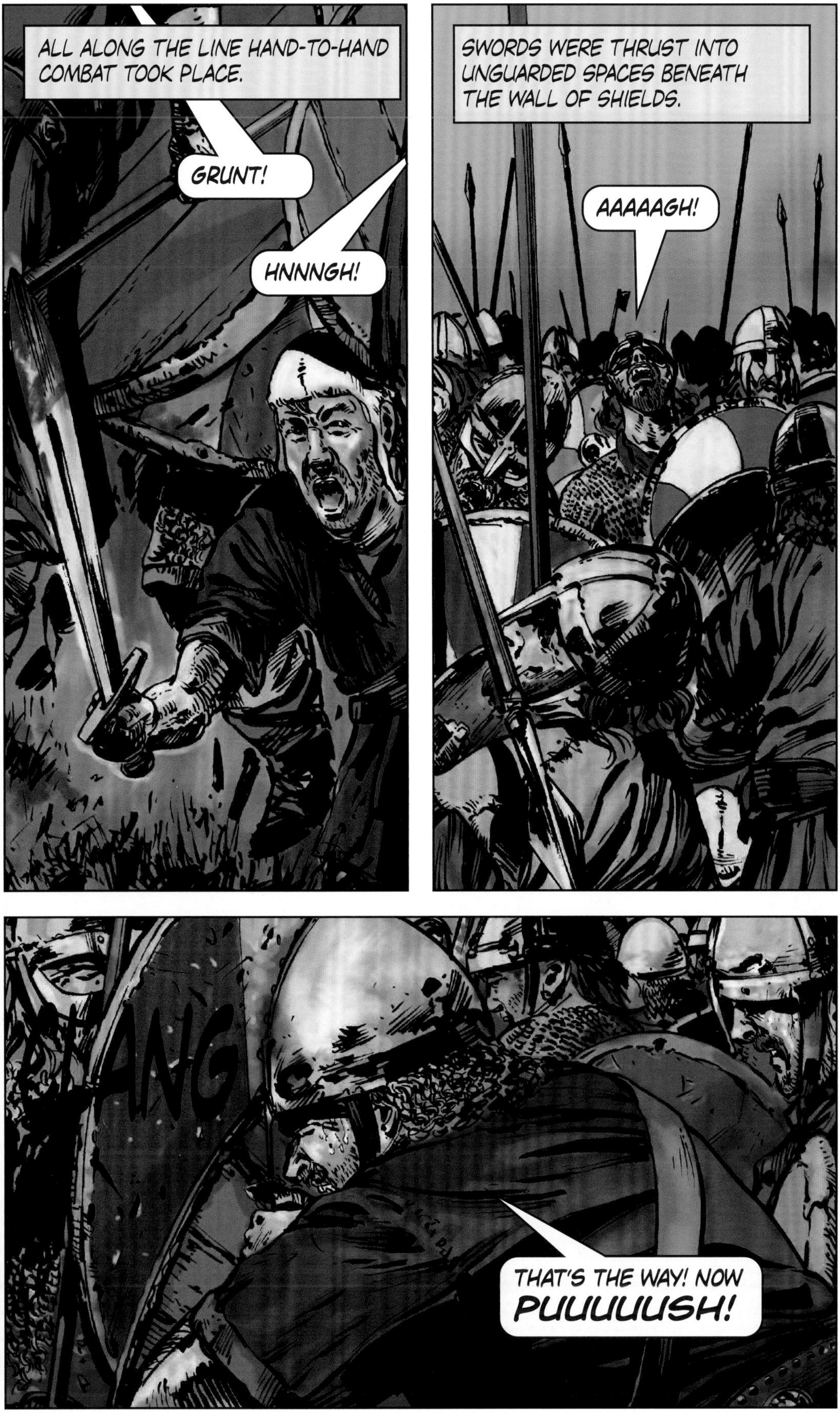
ALL ALONG THE LINE HAND-TO-HAND COMBAT TOOK PLACE.
GRUNT!
HNNNGH!
SWORDS WERE THRUST INTO UNGUARDED SPACES BENEATH THE WALL OF SHIELDS.
AAAAAGH!
CLANG
THAT'S THE WAY! NOW **PUUUUUSH!**

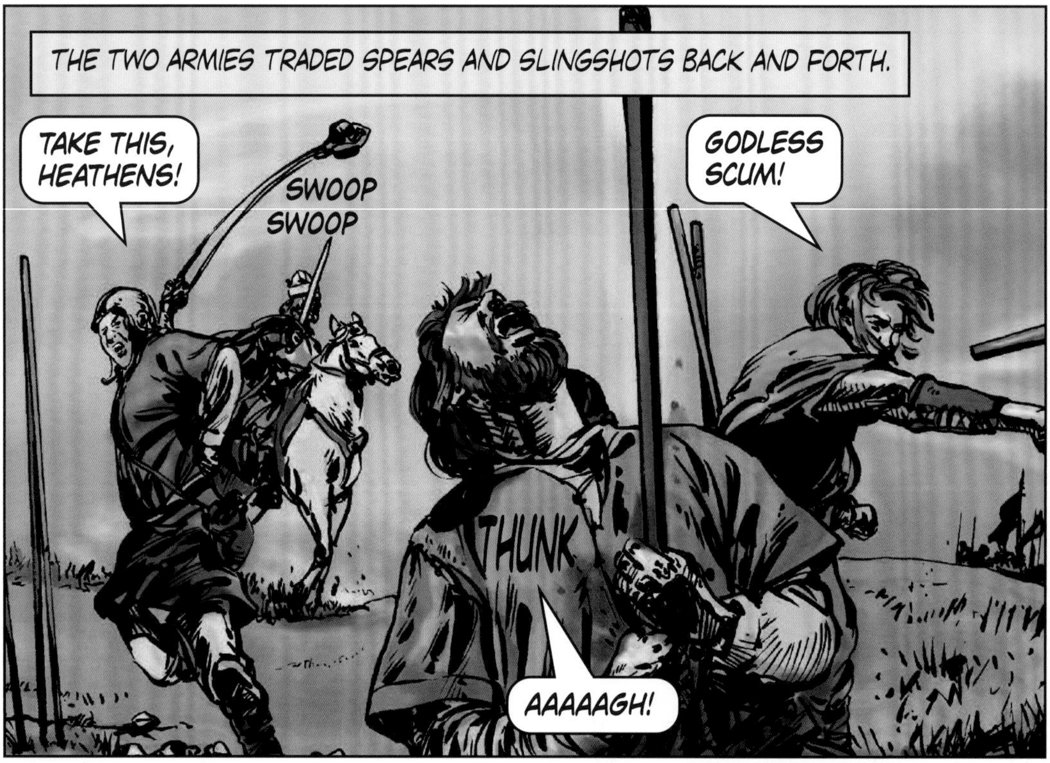
THE TWO ARMIES TRADED SPEARS AND SLINGSHOTS BACK AND FORTH.
TAKE THIS, HEATHENS!
SWOOP SWOOP
GODLESS SCUM!
THUNK
AAAAAGH!

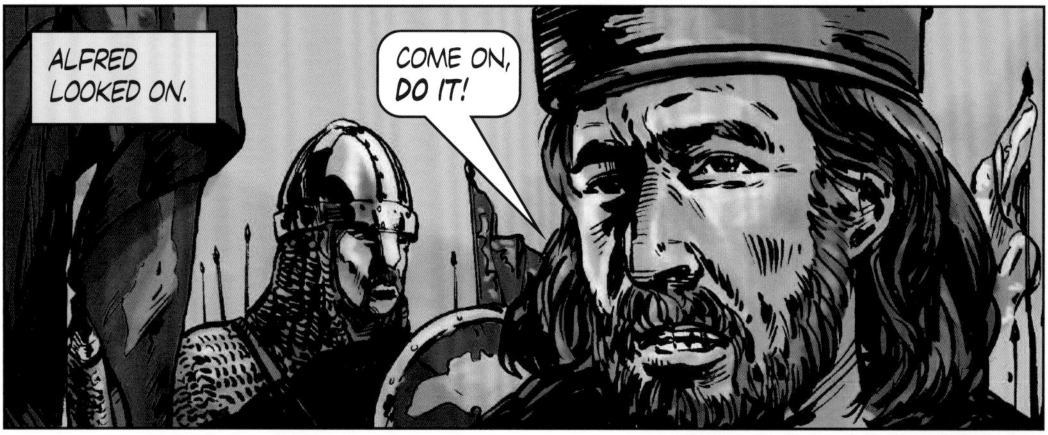
ALFRED LOOKED ON.
COME ON, DO IT!

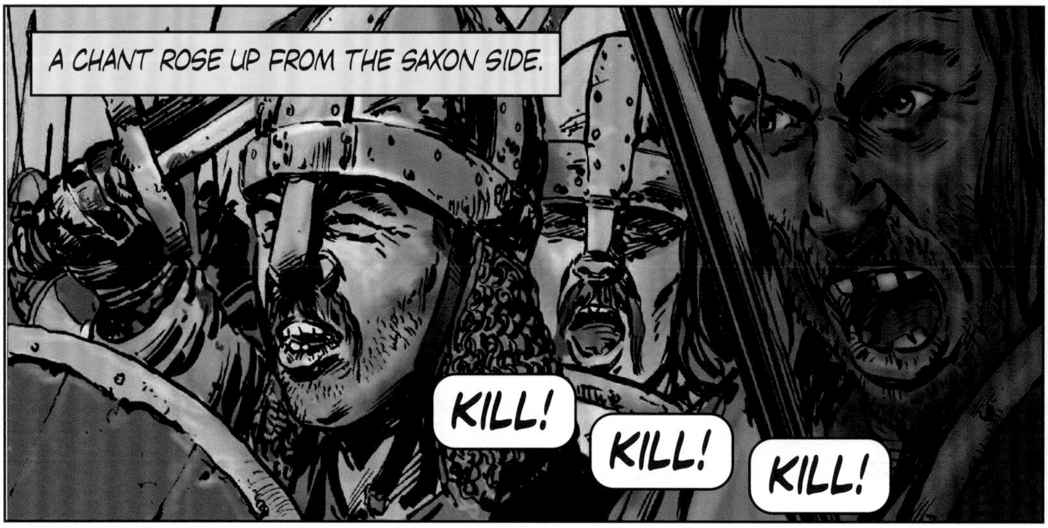
A CHANT ROSE UP FROM THE SAXON SIDE.
KILL!
KILL!
KILL!

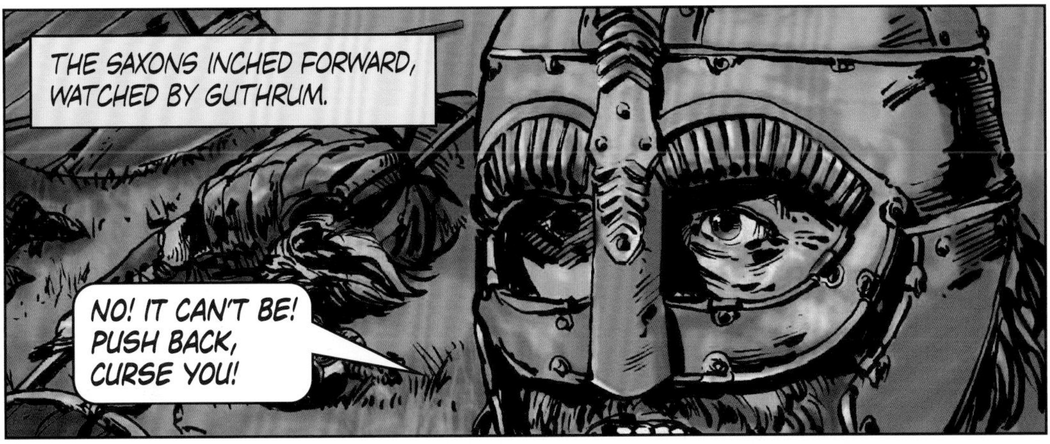
THE SAXONS INCHED FORWARD, WATCHED BY GUTHRUM.
NO! IT CAN'T BE! PUSH BACK, CURSE YOU!

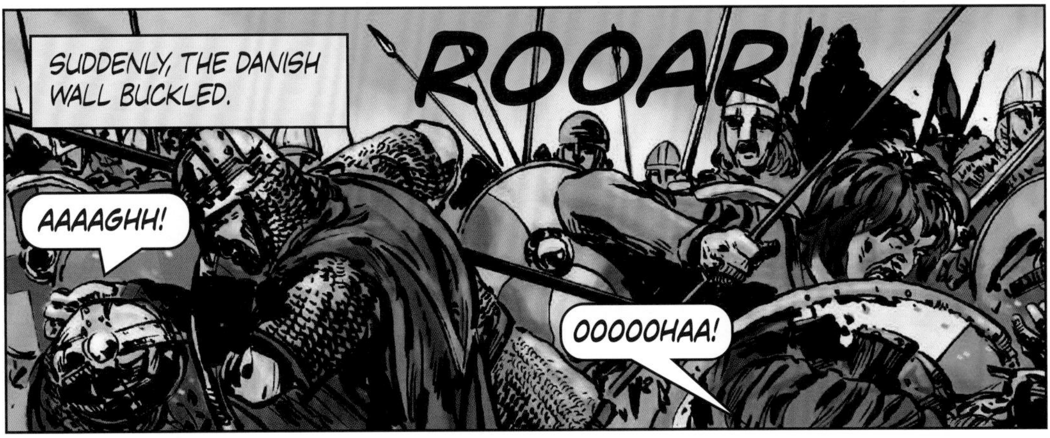
SUDDENLY, THE DANISH WALL BUCKLED.
ROOAR!
AAAAGHH!
OOOOOHAA!

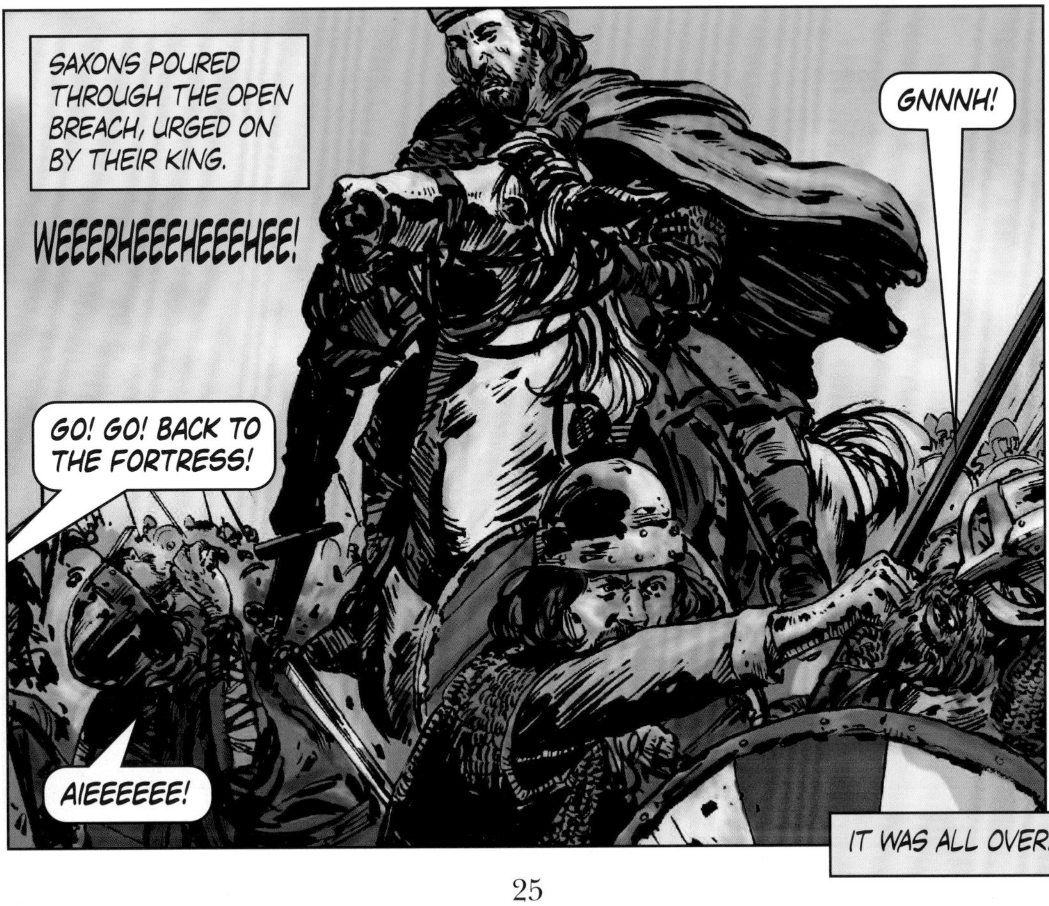
SAXONS POURED THROUGH THE OPEN BREACH, URGED ON BY THEIR KING.
GNNNH!
WEEERHEEEHEEEHEE!
GO! GO! BACK TO THE FORTRESS!
AIEEEEEE!
IT WAS ALL OVER.

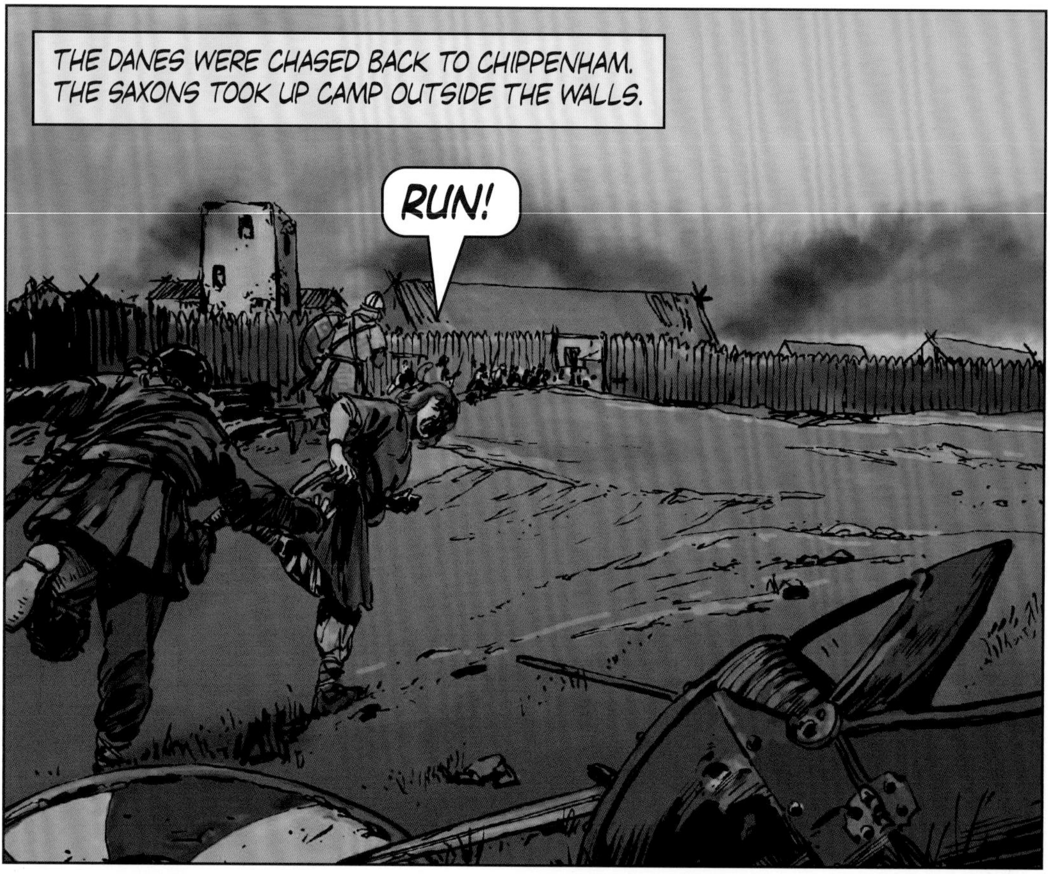
THE DANES WERE CHASED BACK TO CHIPPENHAM. THE SAXONS TOOK UP CAMP OUTSIDE THE WALLS.
RUN!

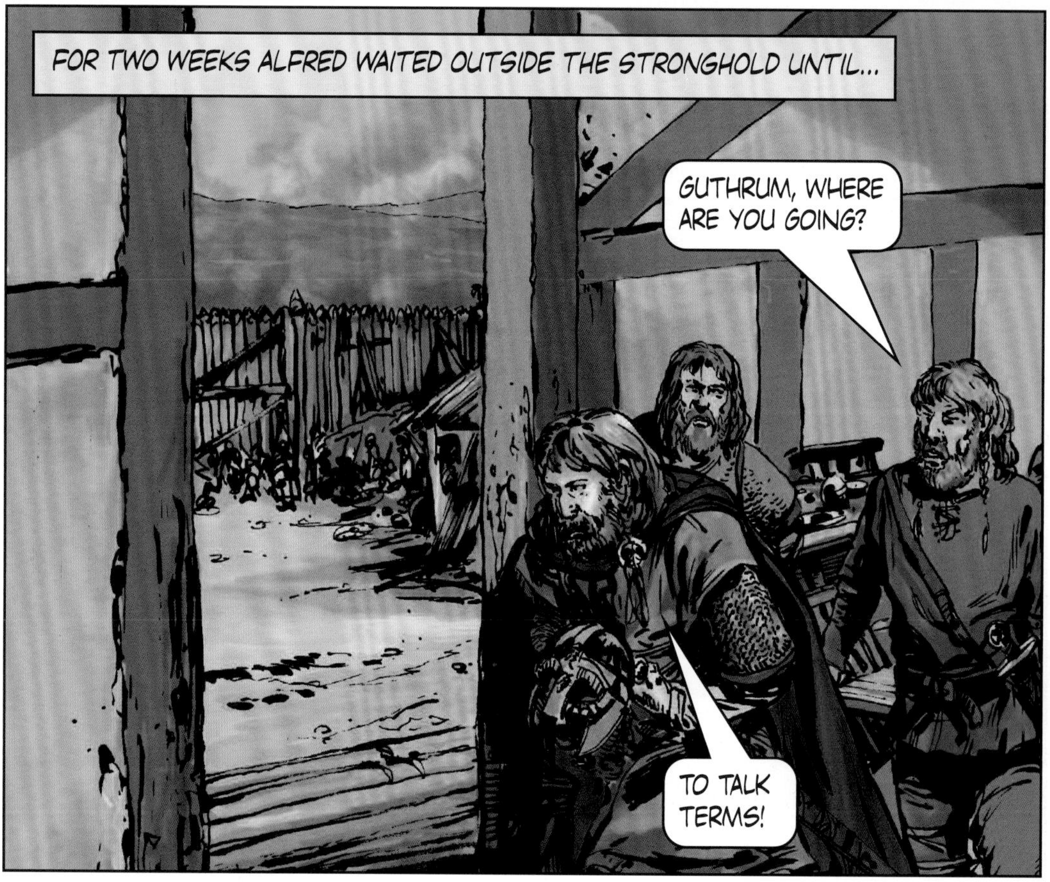
FOR TWO WEEKS ALFRED WAITED OUTSIDE THE STRONGHOLD UNTIL...
GUTHRUM, WHERE ARE YOU GOING?
TO TALK TERMS!

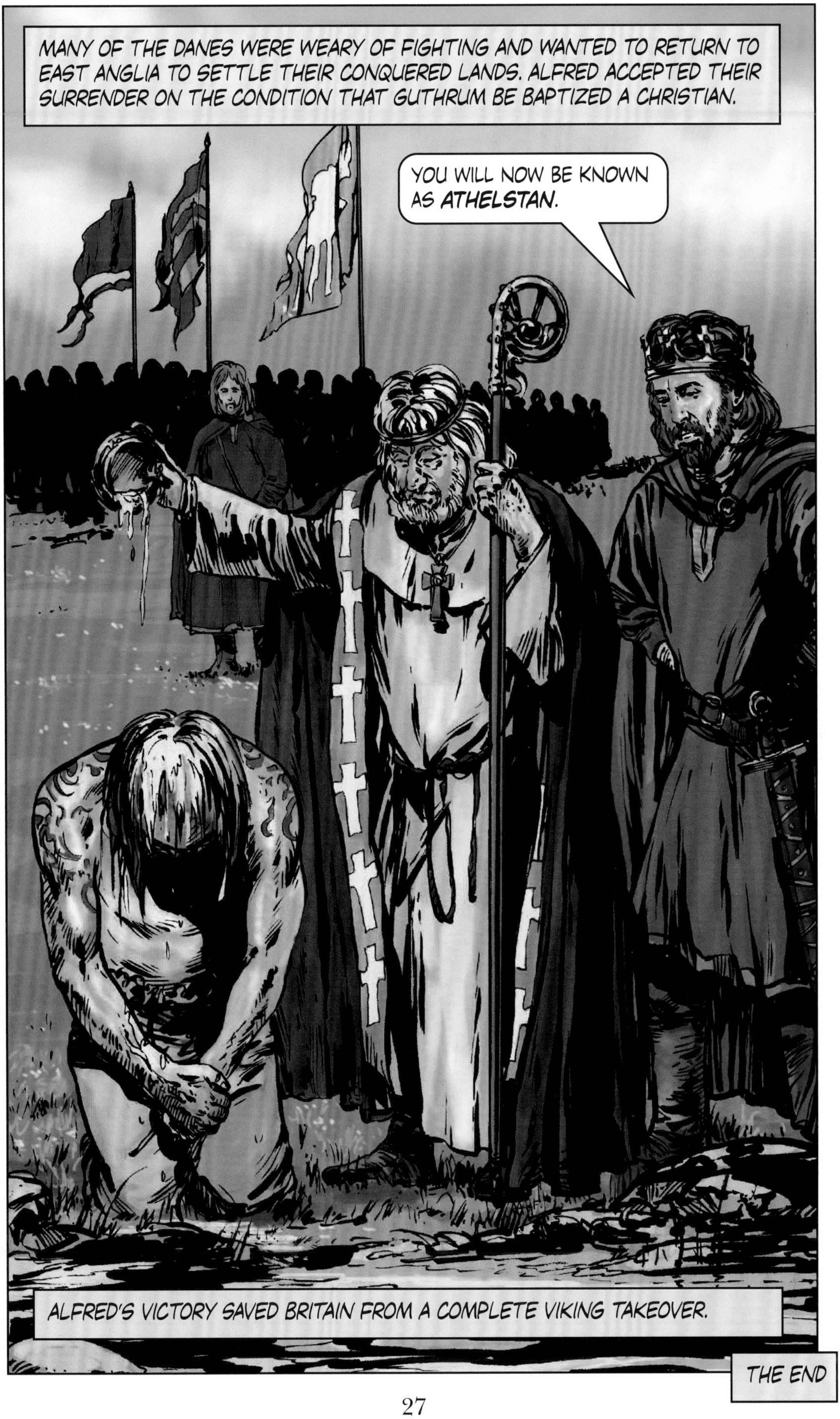
MANY OF THE DANES WERE WEARY OF FIGHTING AND WANTED TO RETURN TO EAST ANGLIA TO SETTLE THEIR CONQUERED LANDS. ALFRED ACCEPTED THEIR SURRENDER ON THE CONDITION THAT GUTHRUM BE BAPTIZED A CHRISTIAN.
YOU WILL NOW BE KNOWN AS ATHELSTAN.
ALFRED'S VICTORY SAVED BRITAIN FROM A COMPLETE VIKING TAKEOVER.
THE END

The Battle of Hastings

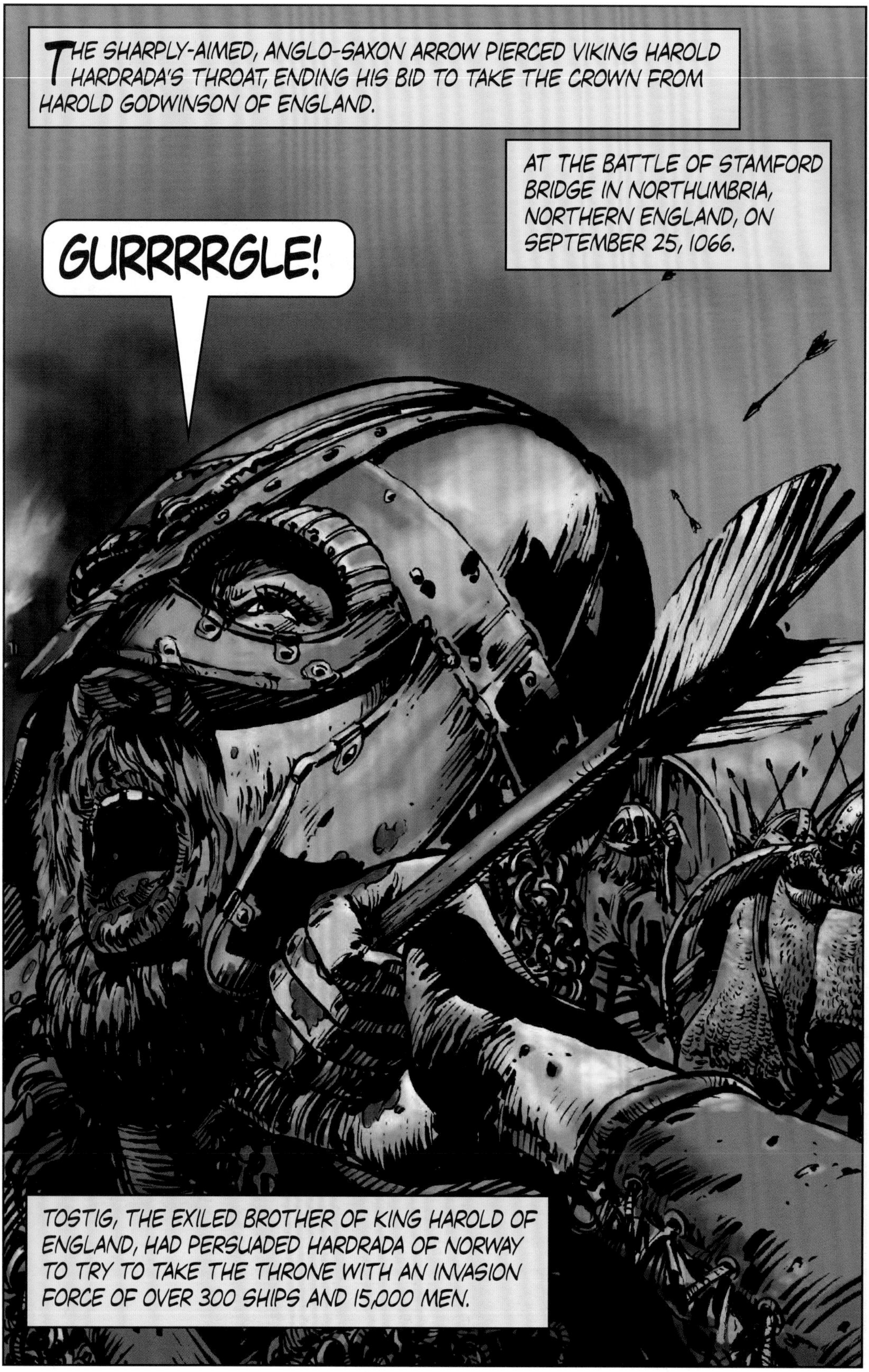
THE SHARPLY-AIMED, ANGLO-SAXON ARROW PIERCED VIKING HAROLD HARDRADA'S THROAT, ENDING HIS BID TO TAKE THE CROWN FROM HAROLD GODWINSON OF ENGLAND.
AT THE BATTLE OF STAMFORD BRIDGE IN NORTHUMBRIA, NORTHERN ENGLAND, ON SEPTEMBER 25, 1066.
GURRRRGLE!
TOSTIG, THE EXILED BROTHER OF KING HAROLD OF ENGLAND, HAD PERSUADED HARDRADA OF NORWAY TO TRY TO TAKE THE THRONE WITH AN INVASION FORCE OF OVER 300 SHIPS AND 15,000 MEN.

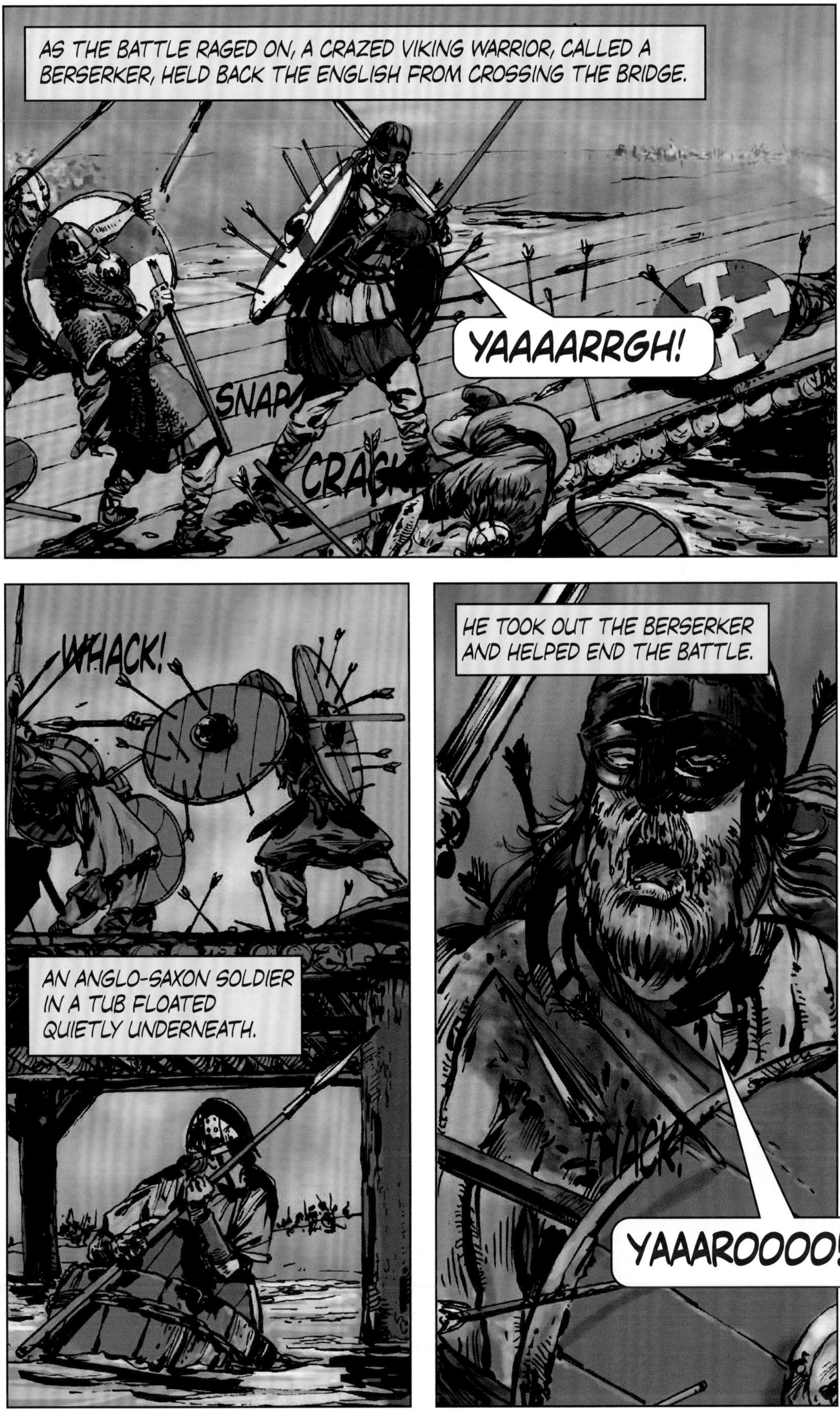
AS THE BATTLE RAGED ON, A CRAZED VIKING WARRIOR, CALLED A BERSERKER, HELD BACK THE ENGLISH FROM CROSSING THE BRIDGE.
YAAAARRGH!
SNAP
CRACK
WHACK!
AN ANGLO-SAXON SOLDIER IN A TUB FLOATED QUIETLY UNDERNEATH.
HE TOOK OUT THE BERSERKER AND HELPED END THE BATTLE.
YAAAROOOO!

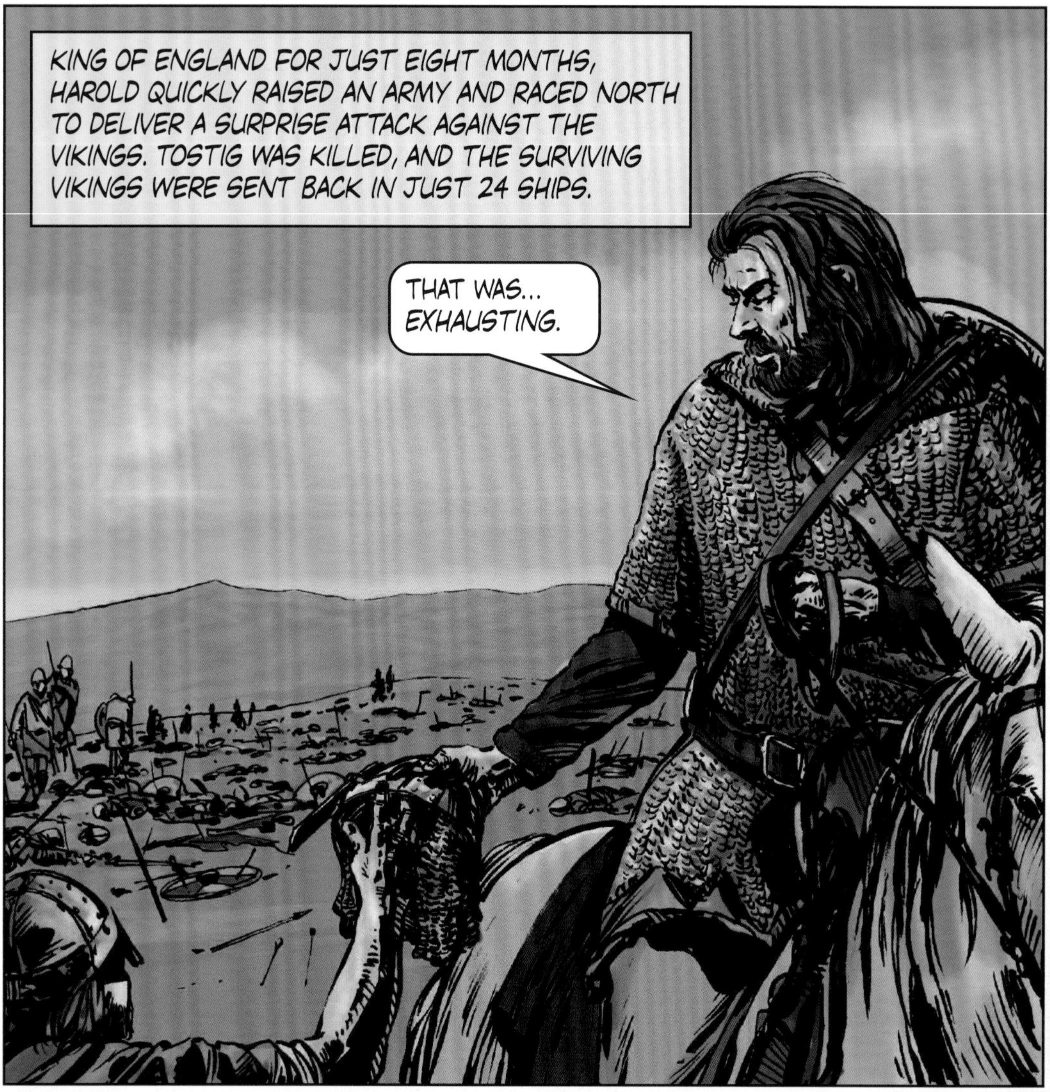
KING OF ENGLAND FOR JUST EIGHT MONTHS, HAROLD QUICKLY RAISED AN ARMY AND RACED NORTH TO DELIVER A SURPRISE ATTACK AGAINST THE VIKINGS. TOSTIG WAS KILLED, AND THE SURVIVING VIKINGS WERE SENT BACK IN JUST 24 SHIPS.
THAT WAS... EXHAUSTING.

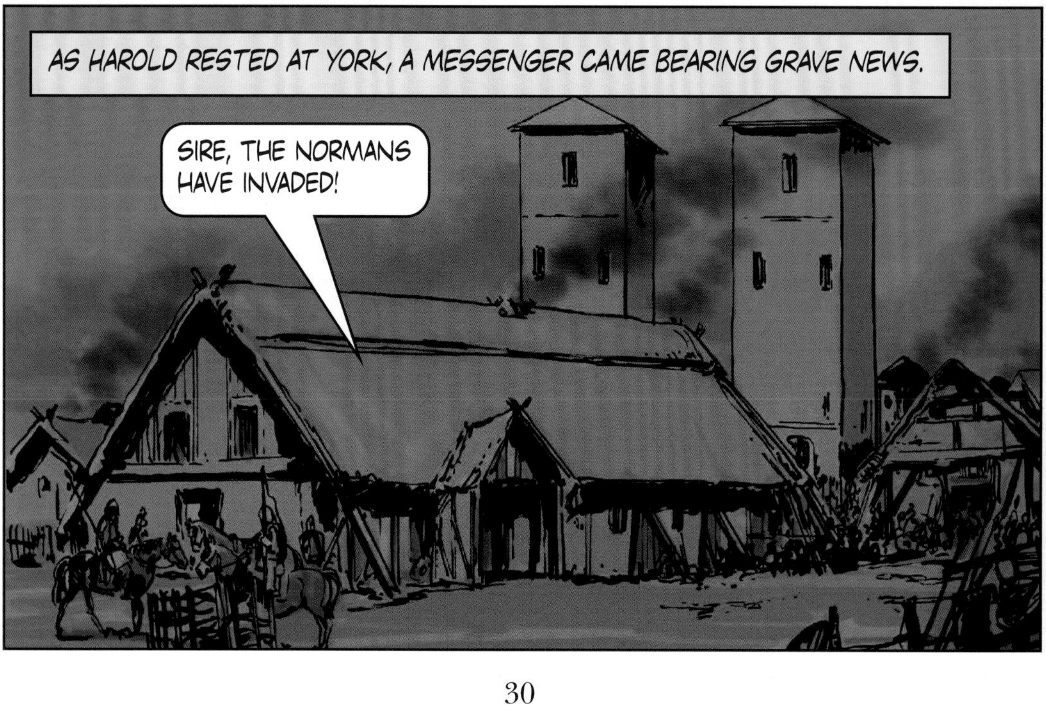
AS HAROLD RESTED AT YORK, A MESSENGER CAME BEARING GRAVE NEWS.
SIRE, THE NORMANS HAVE INVADED!

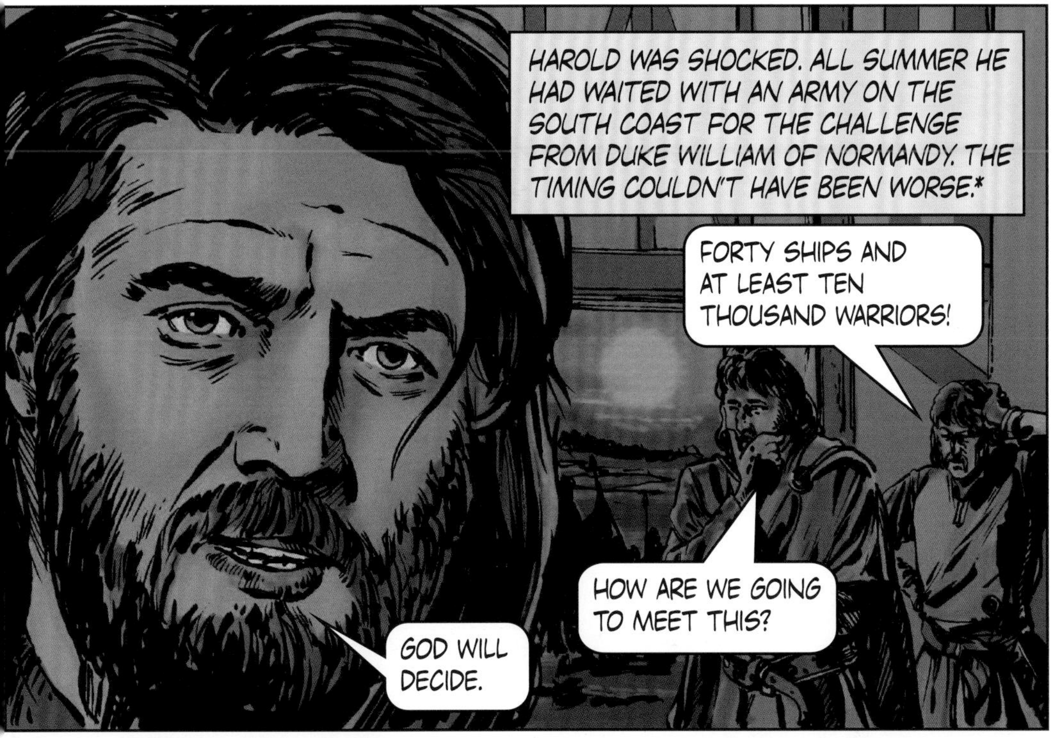
HAROLD WAS SHOCKED. ALL SUMMER HE HAD WAITED WITH AN ARMY ON THE SOUTH COAST FOR THE CHALLENGE FROM DUKE WILLIAM OF NORMANDY. THE TIMING COULDN'T HAVE BEEN WORSE.*
FORTY SHIPS AND AT LEAST TEN THOUSAND WARRIORS!
HOW ARE WE GOING TO MEET THIS?
GOD WILL DECIDE.

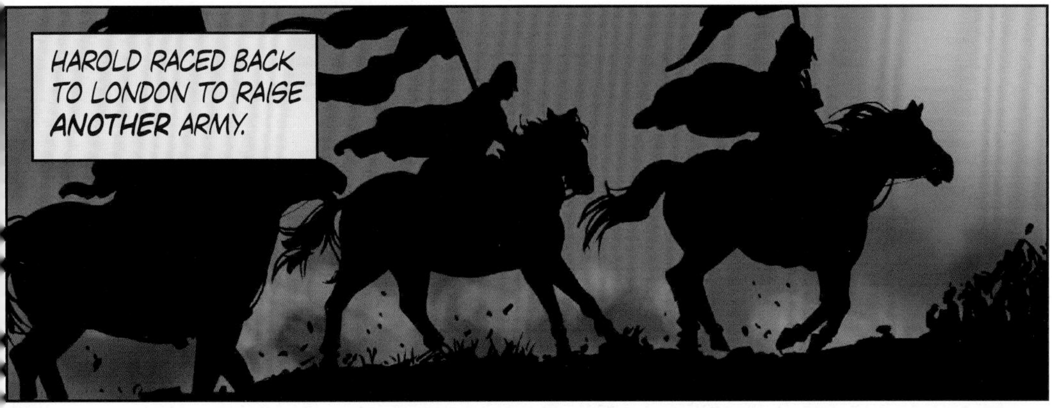
HAROLD RACED BACK TO LONDON TO RAISE **ANOTHER** ARMY.

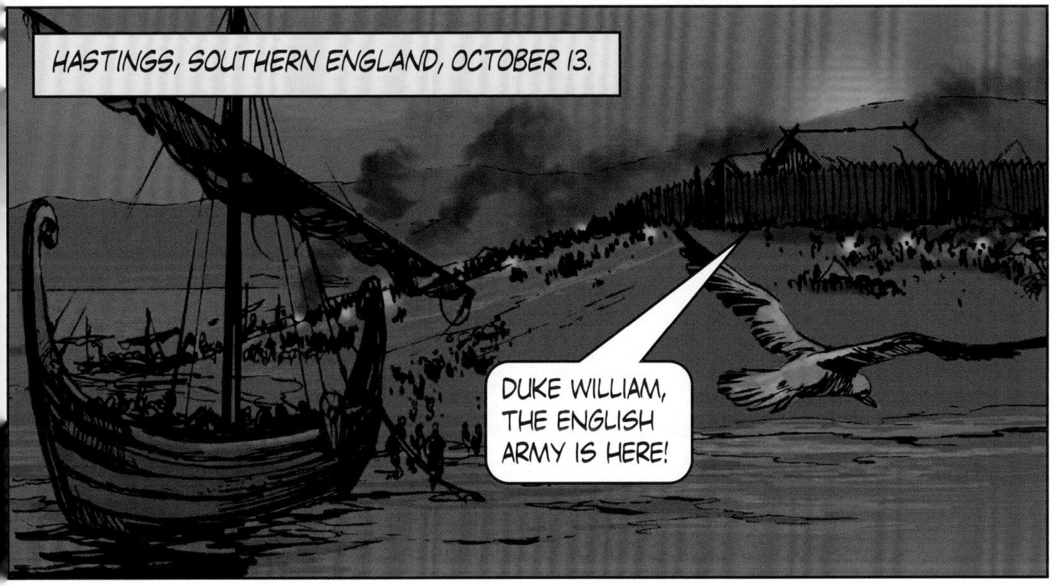
HASTINGS, SOUTHERN ENGLAND, OCTOBER 13.
DUKE WILLIAM, THE ENGLISH ARMY IS HERE!

*FOR MORE ABOUT THIS, SEE PAGE 7.

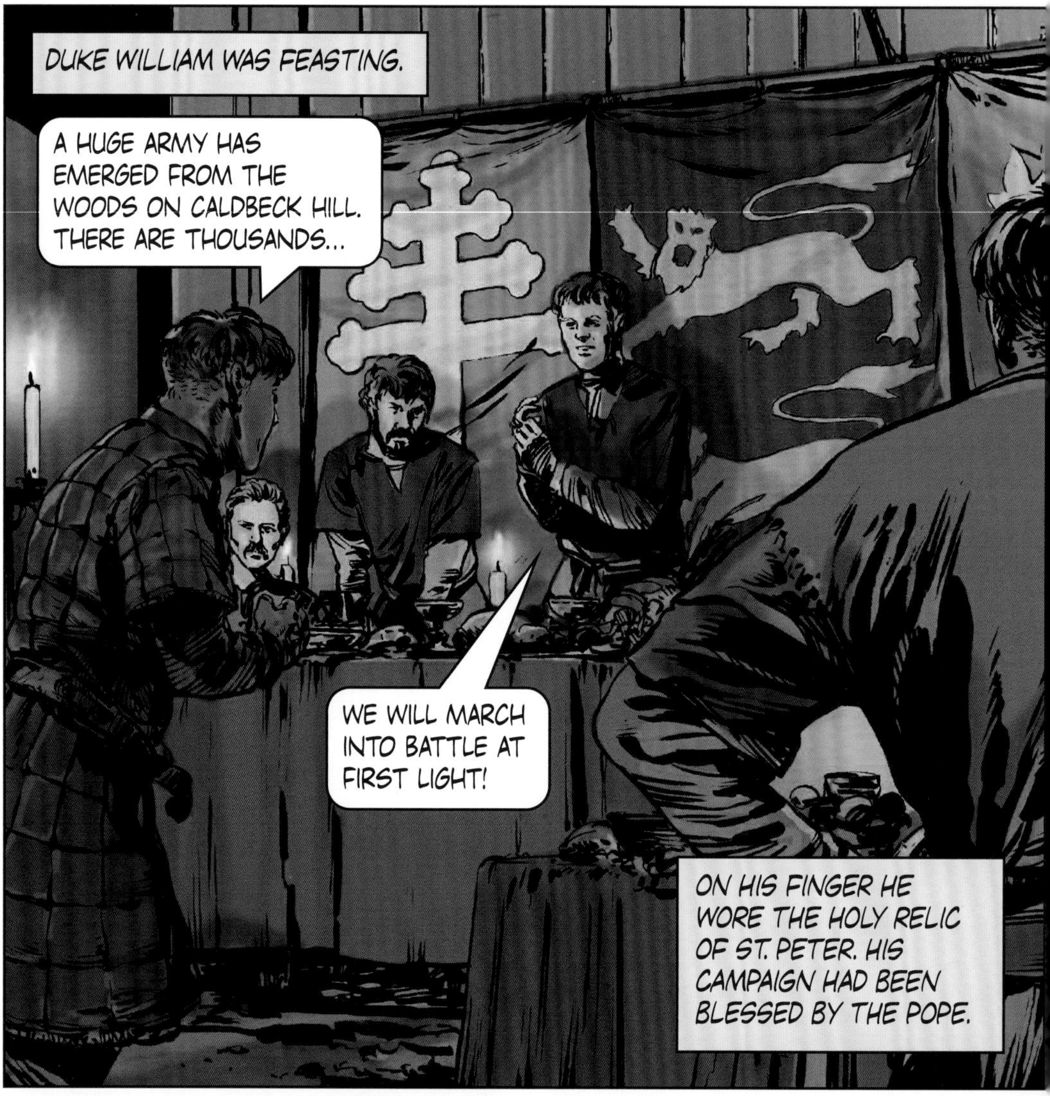
DUKE WILLIAM WAS FEASTING.
A HUGE ARMY HAS EMERGED FROM THE WOODS ON CALDBECK HILL. THERE ARE THOUSANDS...
WE WILL MARCH INTO BATTLE AT FIRST LIGHT!
ON HIS FINGER HE WORE THE HOLY RELIC OF ST. PETER. HIS CAMPAIGN HAD BEEN BLESSED BY THE POPE.

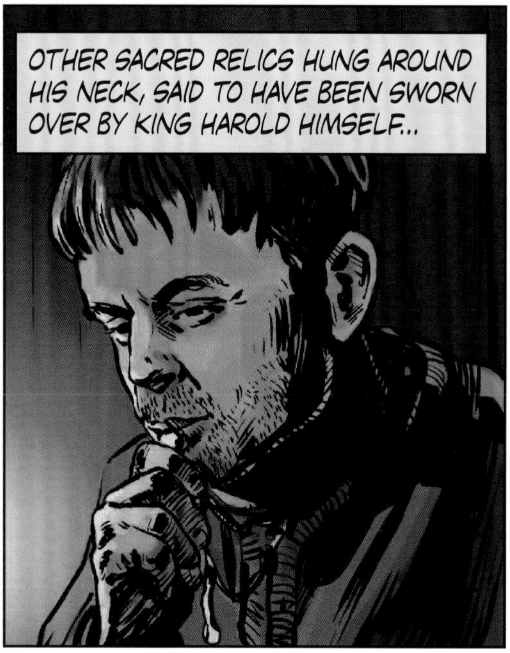
OTHER SACRED RELICS HUNG AROUND HIS NECK, SAID TO HAVE BEEN SWORN OVER BY KING HAROLD HIMSELF...

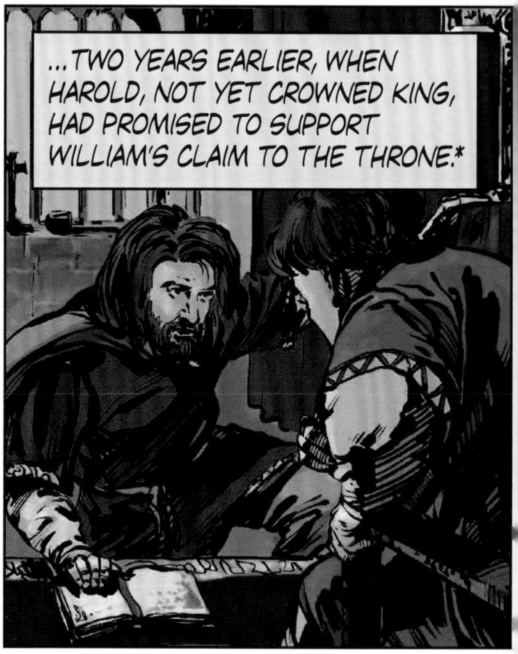
...TWO YEARS EARLIER, WHEN HAROLD, NOT YET CROWNED KING, HAD PROMISED TO SUPPORT WILLIAM'S CLAIM TO THE THRONE.*

*FOR MORE ABOUT THIS SEE PAGE 7.

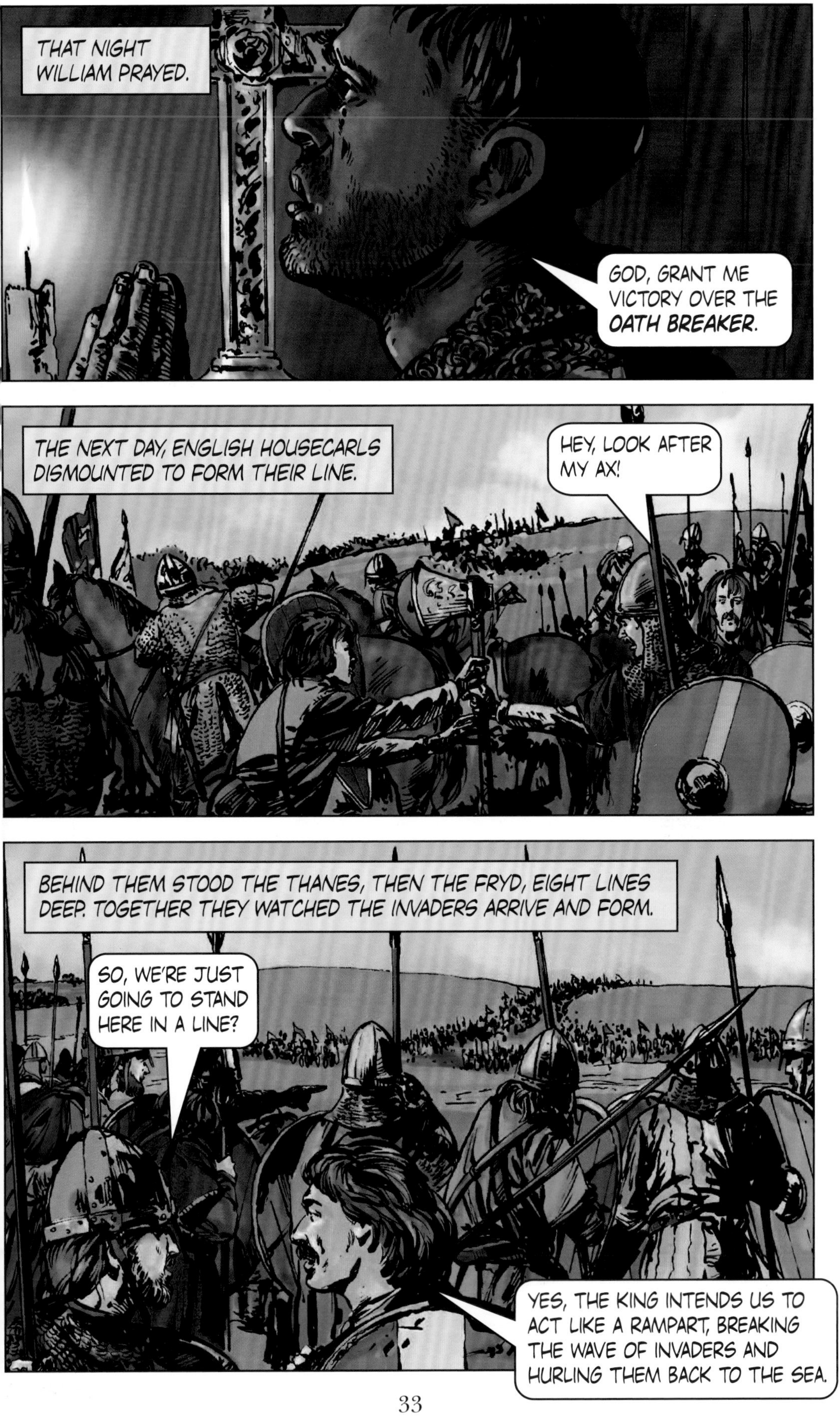
THAT NIGHT WILLIAM PRAYED.
GOD, GRANT ME VICTORY OVER THE **OATH BREAKER**.
THE NEXT DAY, ENGLISH HOUSECARLS DISMOUNTED TO FORM THEIR LINE.
HEY, LOOK AFTER MY AX!
BEHIND THEM STOOD THE THANES, THEN THE FRYD, EIGHT LINES DEEP. TOGETHER THEY WATCHED THE INVADERS ARRIVE AND FORM.
SO, WE'RE JUST GOING TO STAND HERE IN A LINE?
YES, THE KING INTENDS US TO ACT LIKE A RAMPART, BREAKING THE WAVE OF INVADERS AND HURLING THEM BACK TO THE SEA.

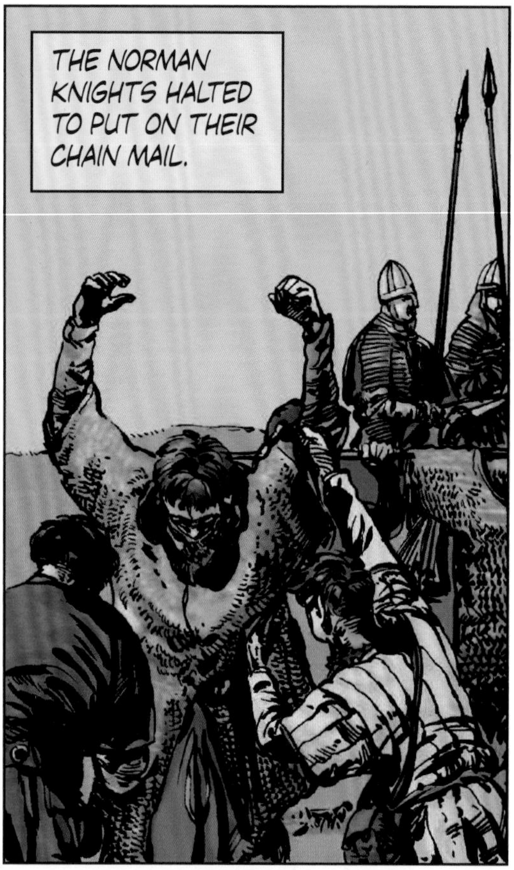
THE NORMAN KNIGHTS HALTED TO PUT ON THEIR CHAIN MAIL.

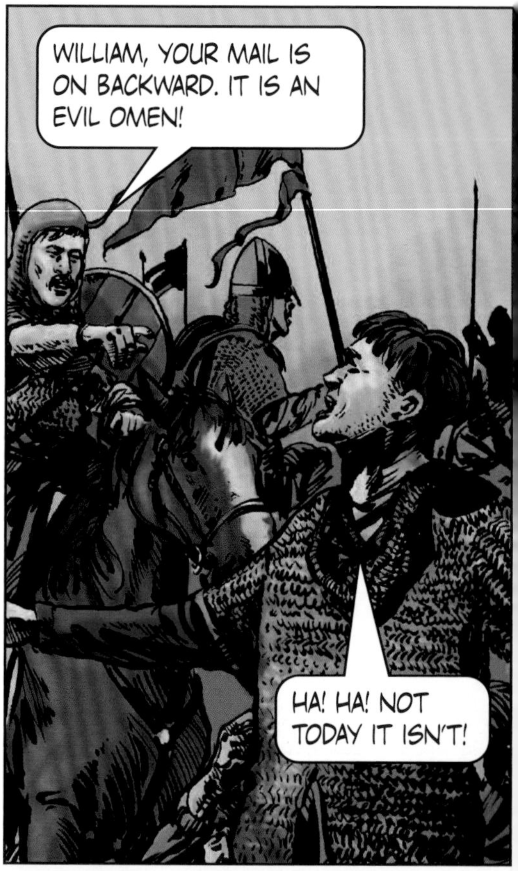
WILLIAM, YOUR MAIL IS ON BACKWARD. IT IS AN EVIL OMEN!
HA! HA! NOT TODAY IT ISN'T!

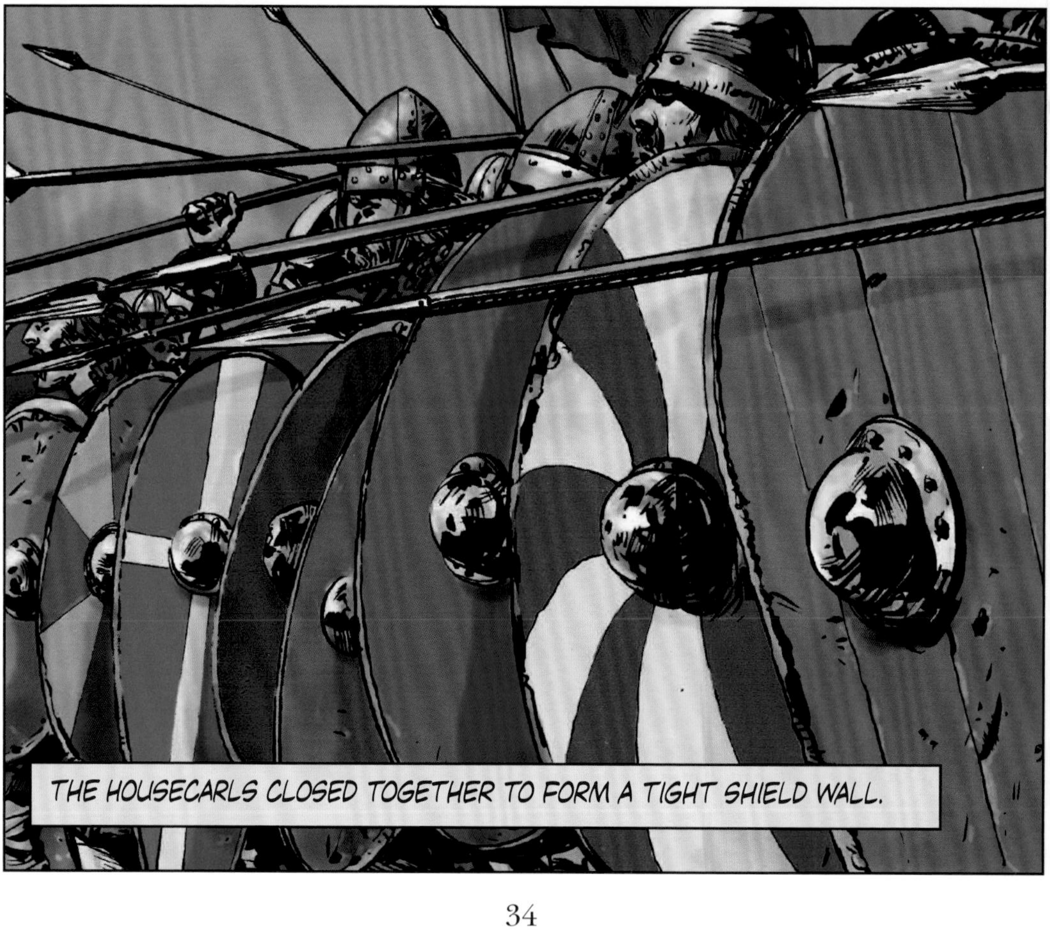
THE HOUSECARLS CLOSED TOGETHER TO FORM A TIGHT SHIELD WALL.

HAROLD'S MEN WERE DEFENDING A RIDGE THAT DROPPED OFF STEEPLY AT BOTH ENDS.

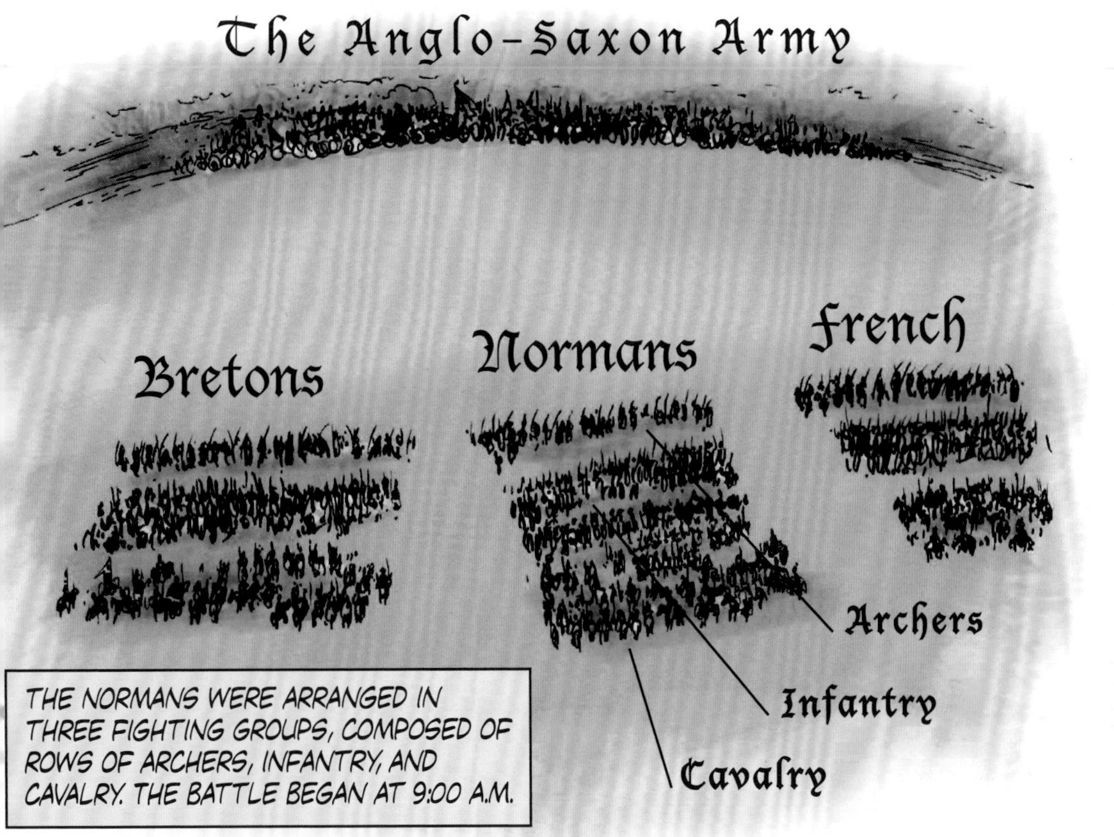
The Anglo-Saxon Army
Bretons
Normans
French
Archers
Infantry
Cavalry
THE NORMANS WERE ARRANGED IN THREE FIGHTING GROUPS, COMPOSED OF ROWS OF ARCHERS, INFANTRY, AND CAVALRY. THE BATTLE BEGAN AT 9:00 A.M.

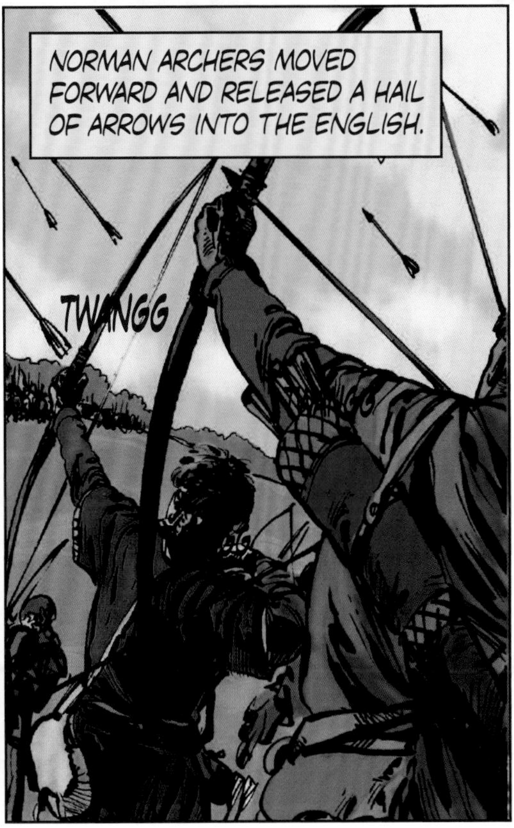
NORMAN ARCHERS MOVED FORWARD AND RELEASED A HAIL OF ARROWS INTO THE ENGLISH.
TWANGG

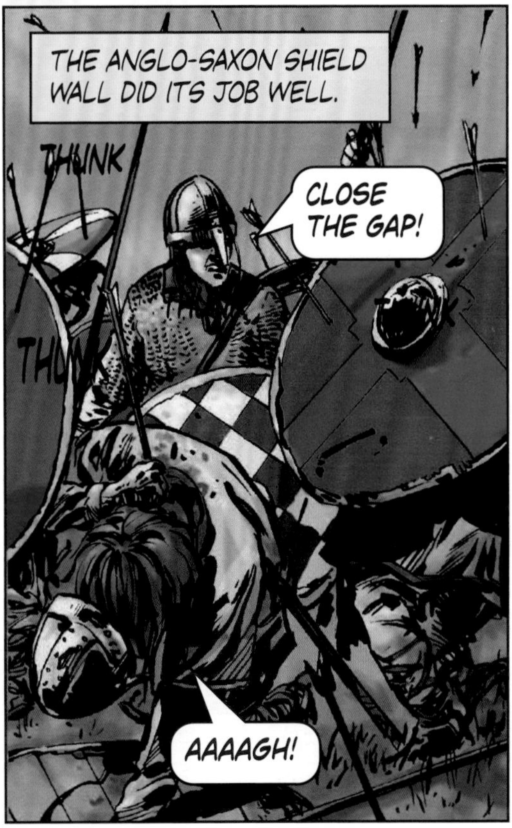
THE ANGLO-SAXON SHIELD WALL DID ITS JOB WELL.
THUNK
CLOSE THE GAP!
AAAAGH!

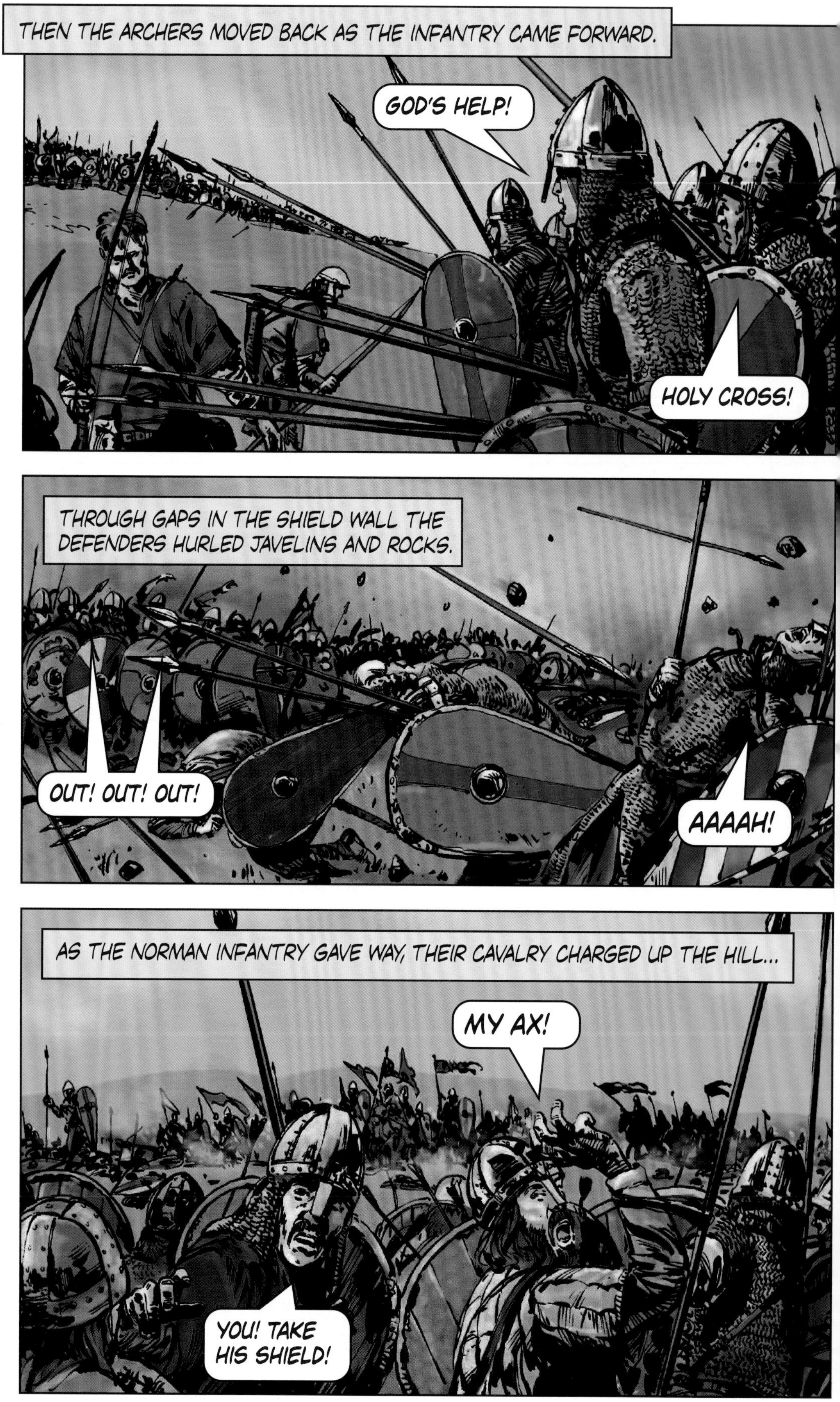
THEN THE ARCHERS MOVED BACK AS THE INFANTRY CAME FORWARD.
GOD'S HELP!
HOLY CROSS!
THROUGH GAPS IN THE SHIELD WALL THE DEFENDERS HURLED JAVELINS AND ROCKS.
OUT! OUT! OUT!
AAAAH!
AS THE NORMAN INFANTRY GAVE WAY, THEIR CAVALRY CHARGED UP THE HILL...
MY AX!
YOU! TAKE HIS SHIELD!

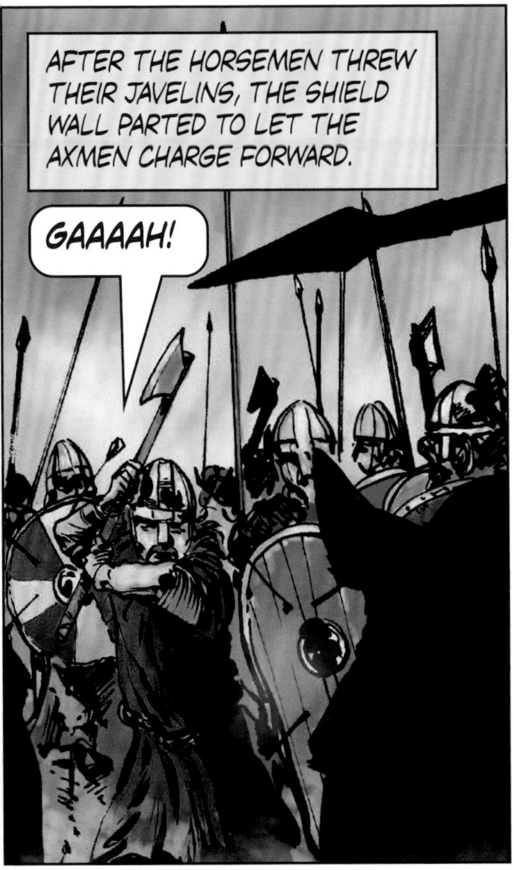
AFTER THE HORSEMEN THREW THEIR JAVELINS, THE SHIELD WALL PARTED TO LET THE AXMEN CHARGE FORWARD.
GAAAAH!

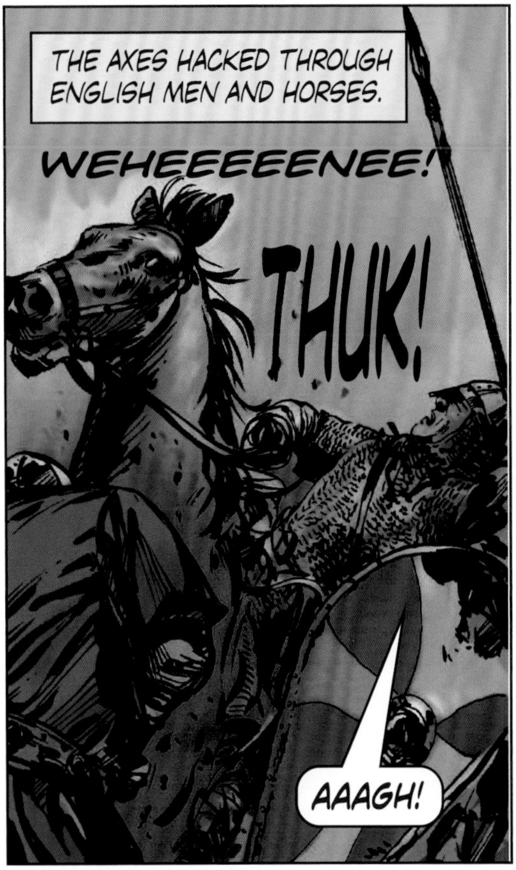
THE AXES HACKED THROUGH ENGLISH MEN AND HORSES.
WEHEEEEEENEE!
THUK!
AAAGH!

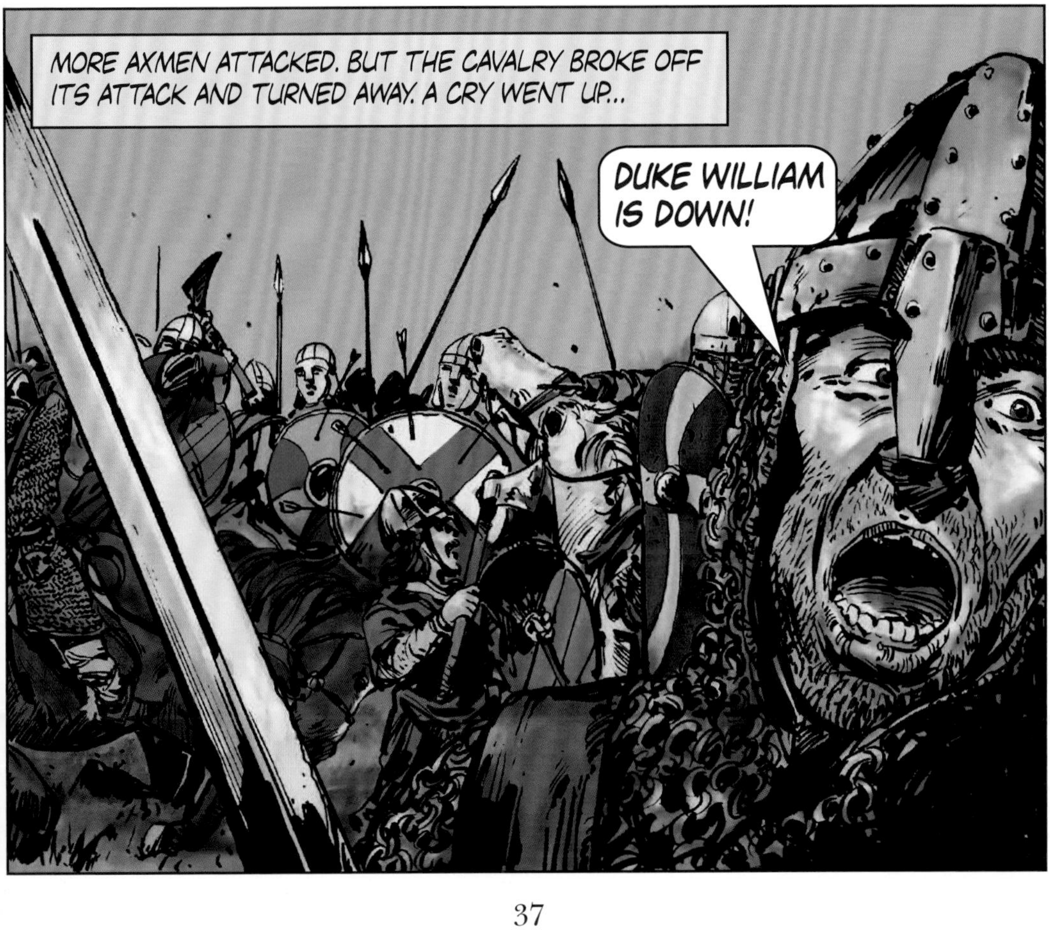
MORE AXMEN ATTACKED. BUT THE CAVALRY BROKE OFF ITS ATTACK AND TURNED AWAY. A CRY WENT UP...
DUKE WILLIAM IS DOWN!

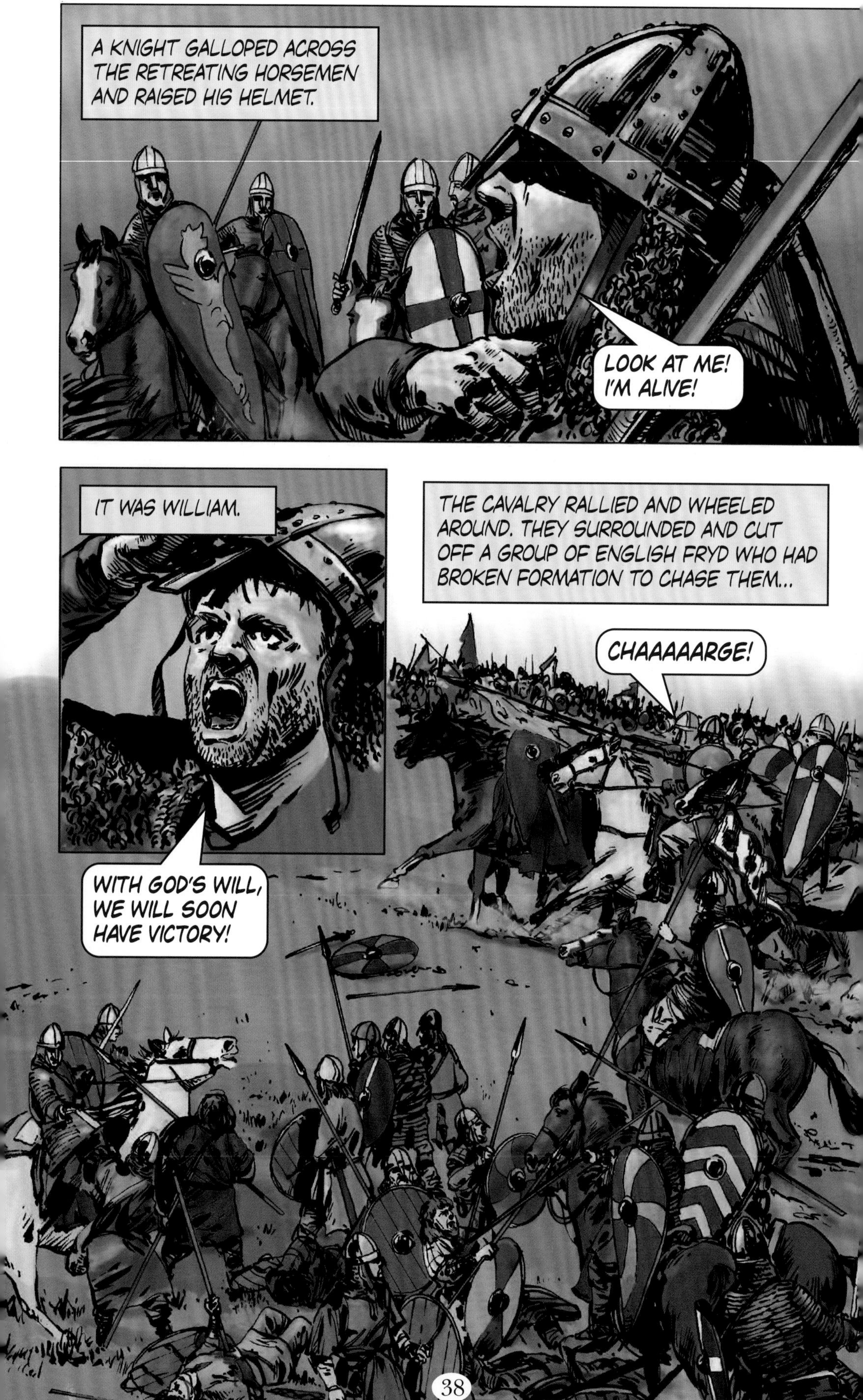
A KNIGHT GALLOPED ACROSS THE RETREATING HORSEMEN AND RAISED HIS HELMET.
LOOK AT ME! I'M ALIVE!
IT WAS WILLIAM.
WITH GOD'S WILL, WE WILL SOON HAVE VICTORY!
THE CAVALRY RALLIED AND WHEELED AROUND. THEY SURROUNDED AND CUT OFF A GROUP OF ENGLISH FRYD WHO HAD BROKEN FORMATION TO CHASE THEM...
CHAAAAARGE!

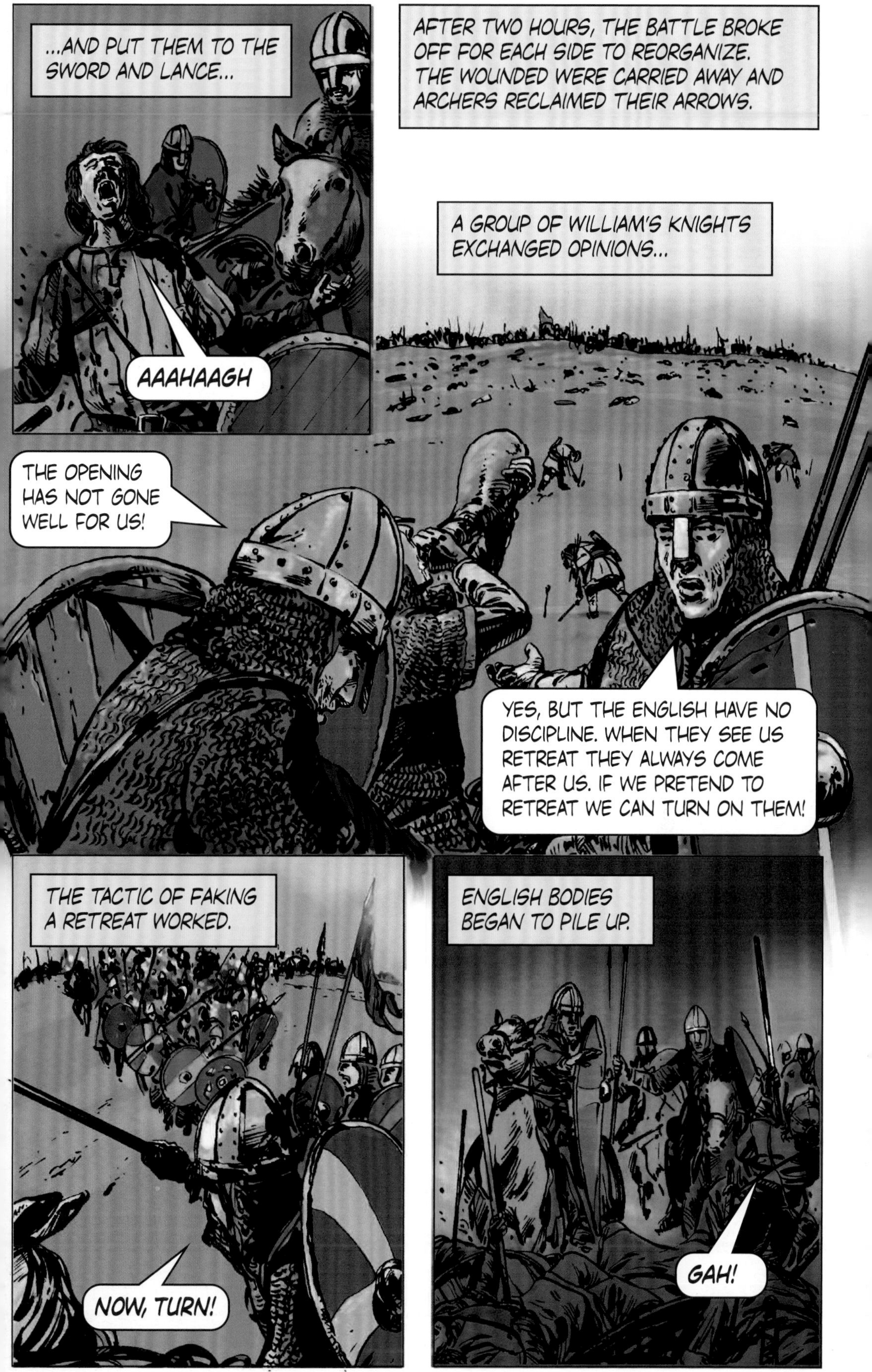
...AND PUT THEM TO THE SWORD AND LANCE...
AAAHAAGH
AFTER TWO HOURS, THE BATTLE BROKE OFF FOR EACH SIDE TO REORGANIZE. THE WOUNDED WERE CARRIED AWAY AND ARCHERS RECLAIMED THEIR ARROWS.
A GROUP OF WILLIAM'S KNIGHTS EXCHANGED OPINIONS...
THE OPENING HAS NOT GONE WELL FOR US!
YES, BUT THE ENGLISH HAVE NO DISCIPLINE. WHEN THEY SEE US RETREAT THEY ALWAYS COME AFTER US. IF WE PRETEND TO RETREAT WE CAN TURN ON THEM!
THE TACTIC OF FAKING A RETREAT WORKED.
NOW, TURN!
ENGLISH BODIES BEGAN TO PILE UP.
GAH!

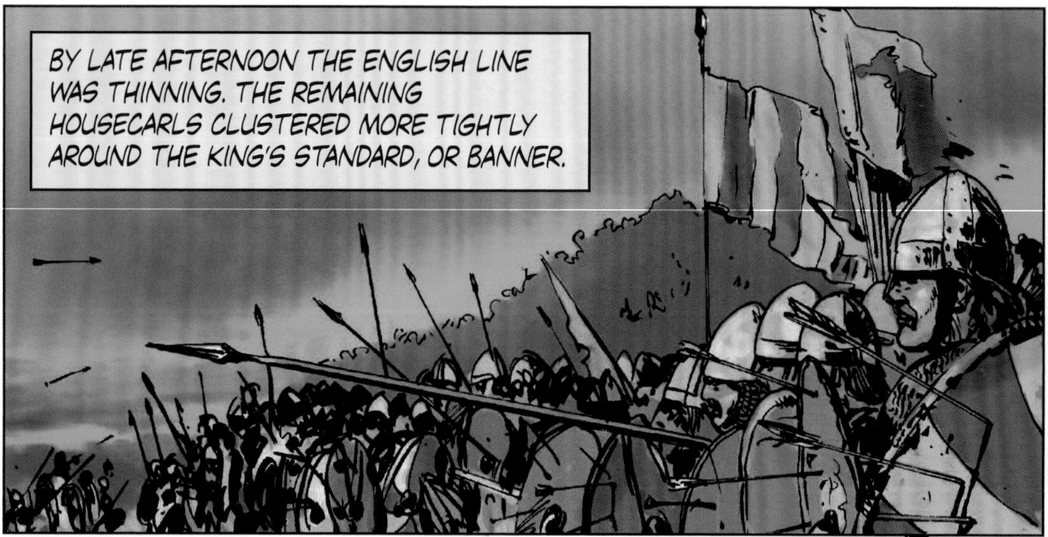
BY LATE AFTERNOON THE ENGLISH LINE WAS THINNING. THE REMAINING HOUSECARLS CLUSTERED MORE TIGHTLY AROUND THE KING'S STANDARD, OR BANNER.

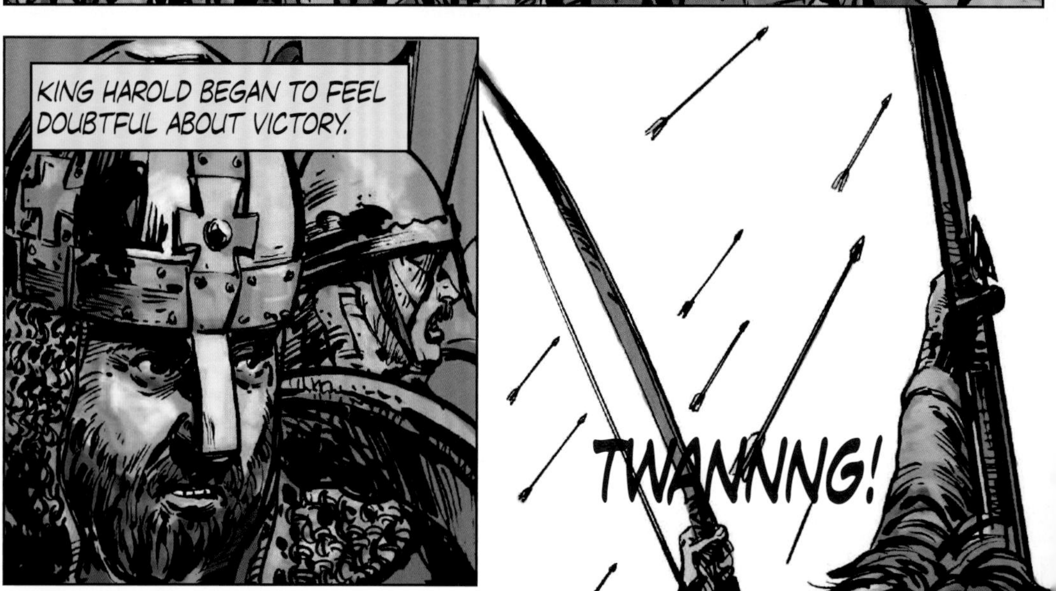
KING HAROLD BEGAN TO FEEL DOUBTFUL ABOUT VICTORY.

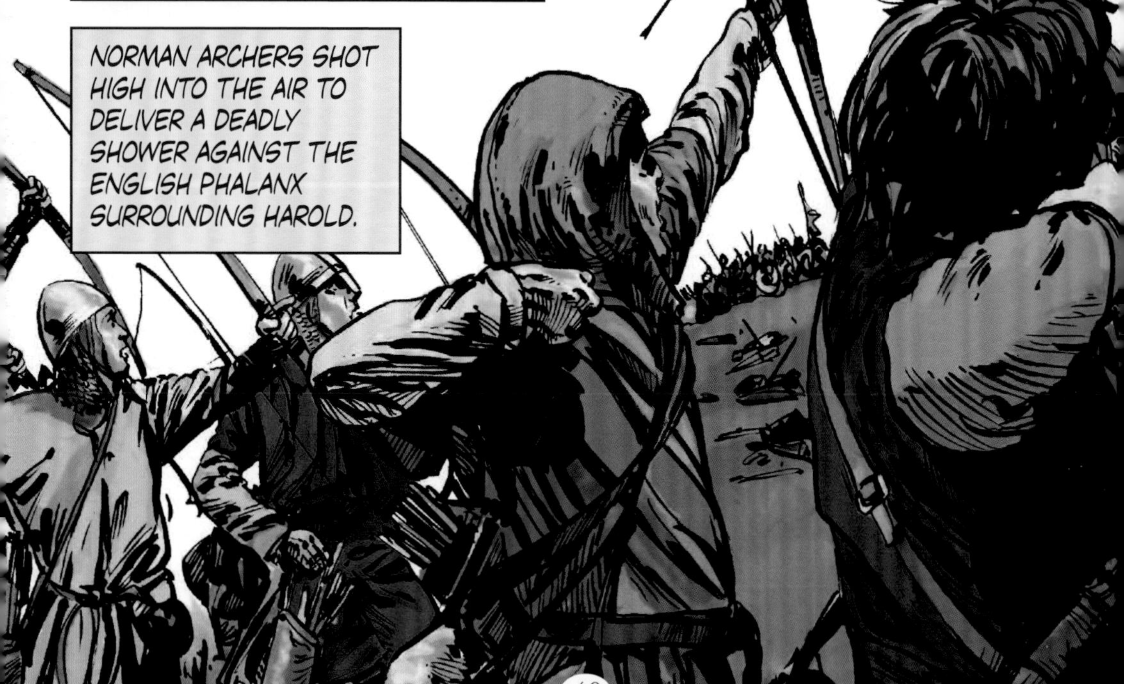
TWANNNG!
NORMAN ARCHERS SHOT HIGH INTO THE AIR TO DELIVER A DEADLY SHOWER AGAINST THE ENGLISH PHALANX SURROUNDING HAROLD.

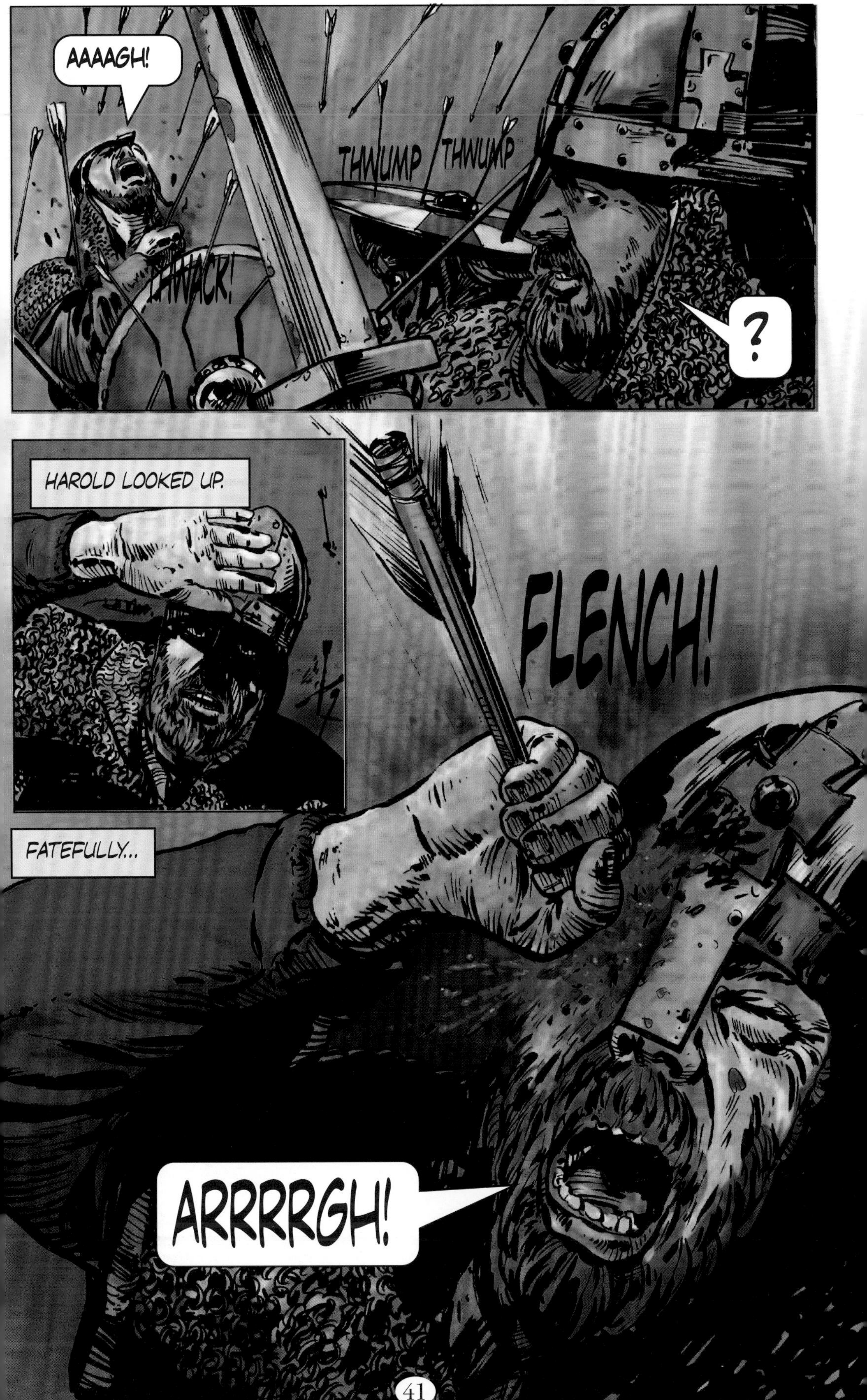
AAAAGH!
THWUMP THWUMP
THWACK!
?
HAROLD LOOKED UP.
FLENCH!
FATEFULLY...
ARRRRGH!

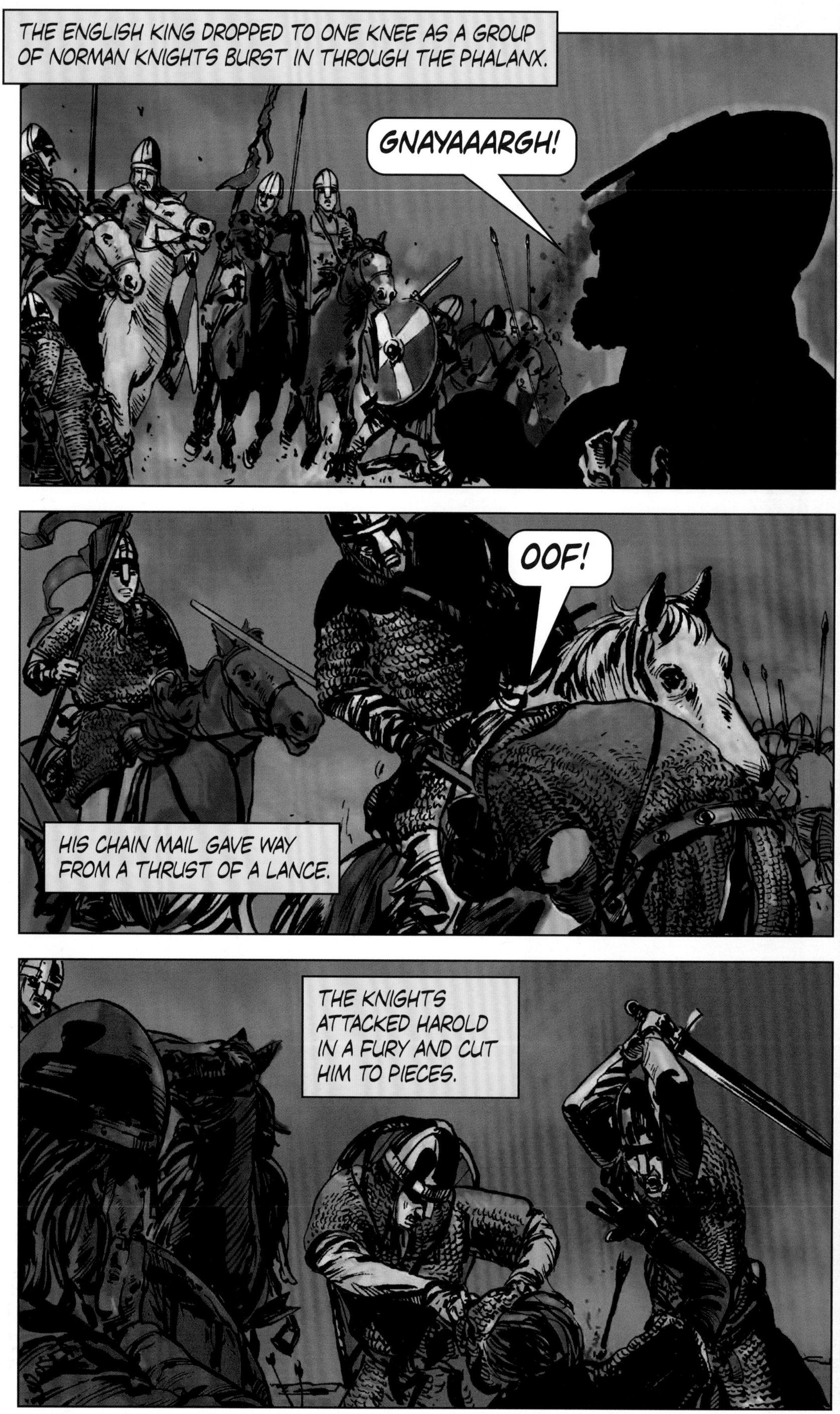
THE ENGLISH KING DROPPED TO ONE KNEE AS A GROUP OF NORMAN KNIGHTS BURST IN THROUGH THE PHALANX.
GNAYAAARGH!
OOF!
HIS CHAIN MAIL GAVE WAY FROM A THRUST OF A LANCE.
THE KNIGHTS ATTACKED HAROLD IN A FURY AND CUT HIM TO PIECES.

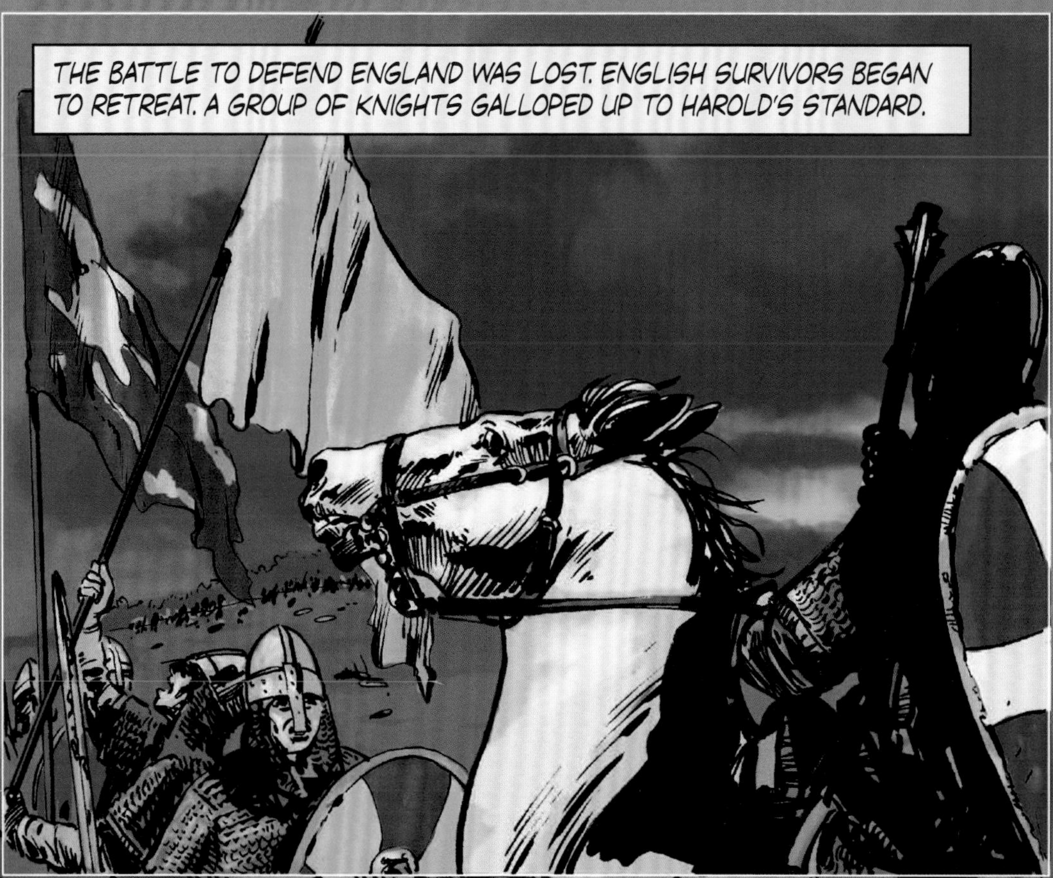
THE BATTLE TO DEFEND ENGLAND WAS LOST. ENGLISH SURVIVORS BEGAN TO RETREAT. A GROUP OF KNIGHTS GALLOPED UP TO HAROLD'S STANDARD.

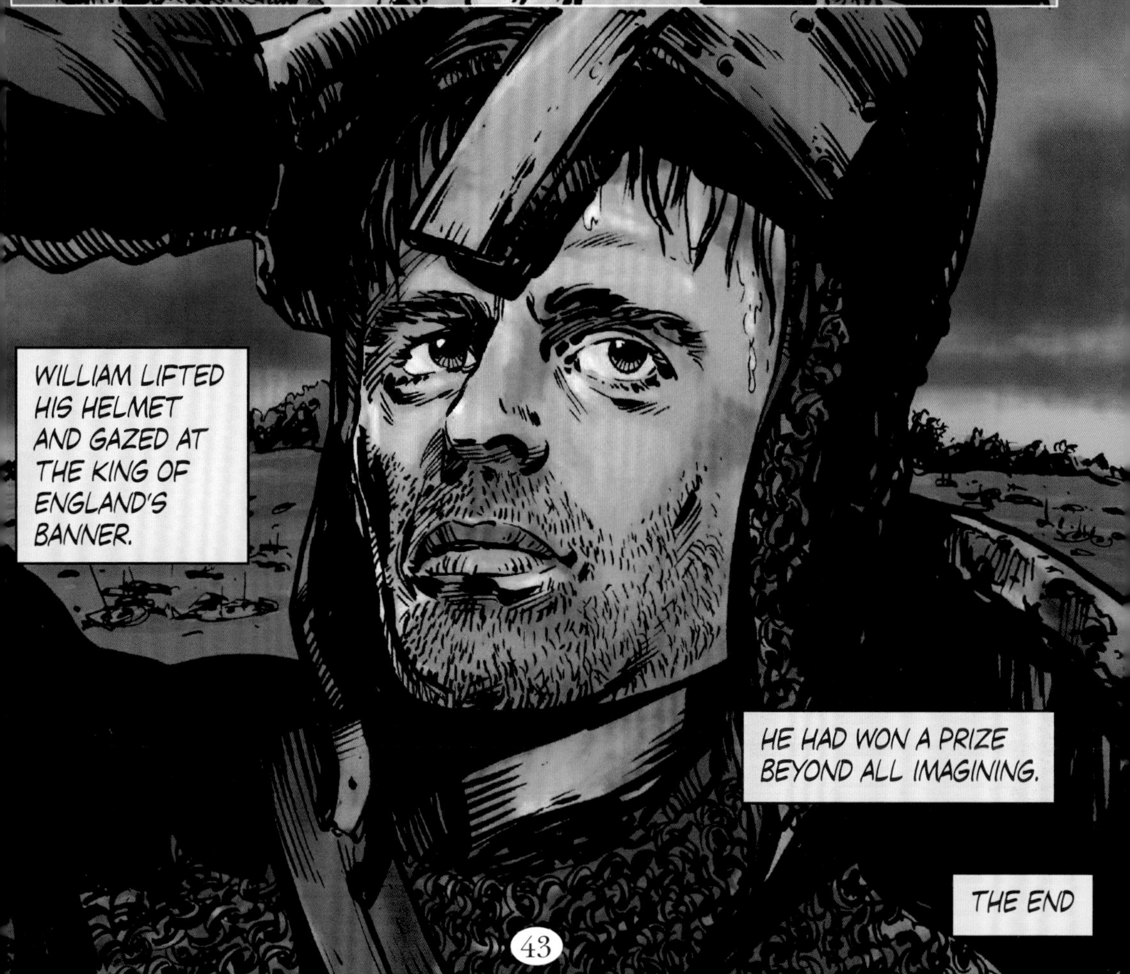
WILLIAM LIFTED HIS HELMET AND GAZED AT THE KING OF ENGLAND'S BANNER.
HE HAD WON A PRIZE BEYOND ALL IMAGINING.
THE END

Changing Rule

We will never know why Harold II rushed into battle so quickly, instead of choosing to wear down the Normans over a longer campaign. With his death, 600 years of Anglo-Saxon rule ended.

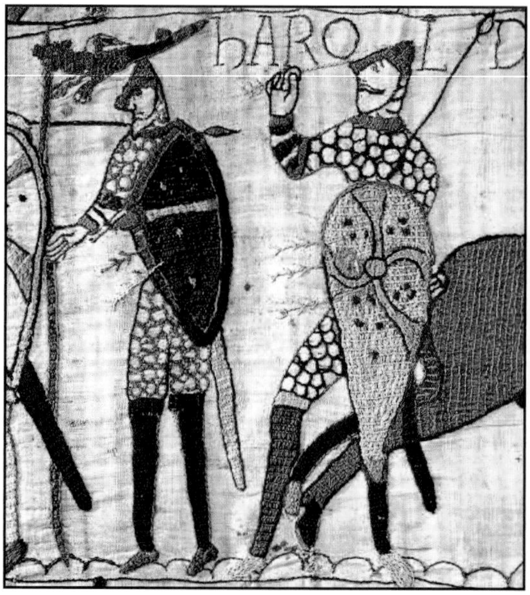

The death of Harold is shown on the Bayeux Tapestry, a monumental embroidery made in 1070 to celebrate William the Conqueror's victory at Hastings.

Spoils of War

After circling London with a tiny force, William I was crowned on December 25, 1066. He had gained the help of his nobles in battle by promising them lands and treasure. His army was also made up of mercenaries who would take plunder as their pay.

Any dreams of ruling a cooperative, peaceful England were lost when William mercilessly seized English land and handed it out to his followers. On great estates and in small villages, the English were made homeless and many starved. Those who complained were thrown into the dungeons of newly-built castles.

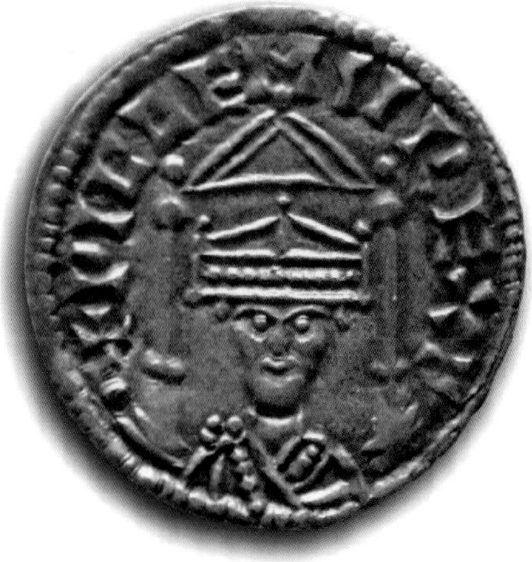

William the Conquerer appears on this 11th-century coin.

Life of a Conquerer

William's rule led to many revolts, but none succeeded. He quickly grew to hate his new kingdom and, after 1075, spent as little time as possible in England. As he grew older he even argued with his son, Robert, who joined forces with Philip, the king of France, instead. Nearly always fighting a battle somewhere, William fell from his horse and died in France in 1087.

THE NORMAN LEGACY

When the Normans took over, wooden palisade forts built on high mounds sprung up across the country. Later, these were rebuilt in stone as residences for the new Norman nobles. These were the first castles of England. William ordered his nobles to supply knights to defend the kingdom. They were very different from the fryd (militia) of the Anglo-Saxons who were mostly farmers.

William ordered the first written survey of all of England's property. Called the Domesday Book, it is a unique record of the times that has survived to this day. The Norman conquest changed England forever.

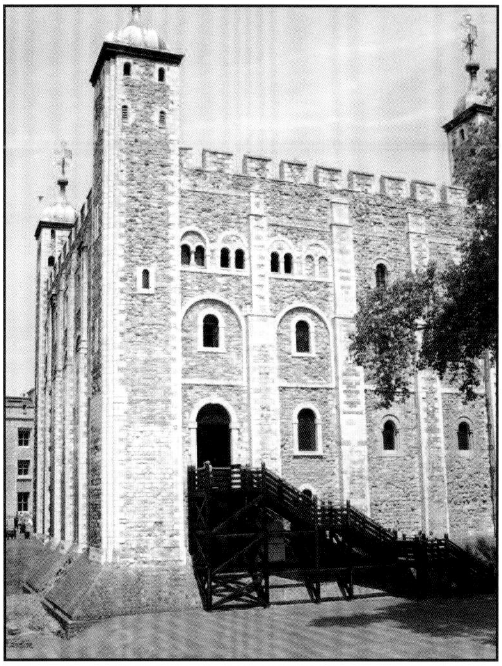

The most famous Norman castle keep, or tower, is the White Tower at the Tower of London, a fortress started in 1075.

The Vikings had settled in Greenland and established themselves as the Rus in eastern Europe—a people who would one day found Russia. They also discovered Iceland and, in 999, became the first Europeans to discover the New World, when Leif Eriksson landed in Newfoundland, Canada, after being blown off course.

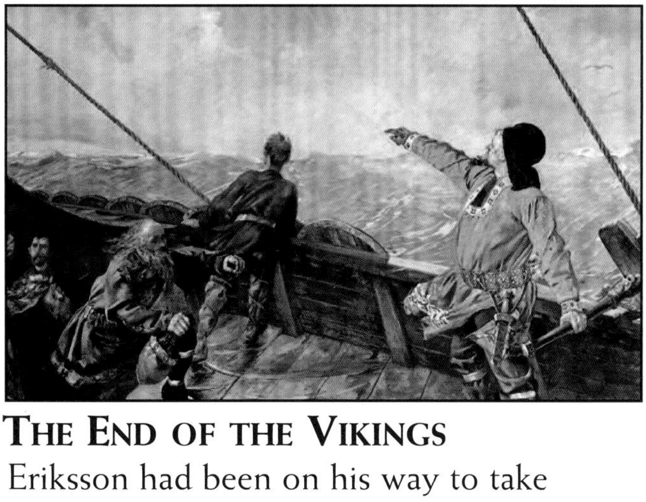

THE END OF THE VIKINGS

Eriksson had been on his way to take Christianity to Greenland. The Viking era ended when the last Vikings converted in 1100. The adventurous seafarers had done more than anyone to change the history of Europe in the Dark Ages.

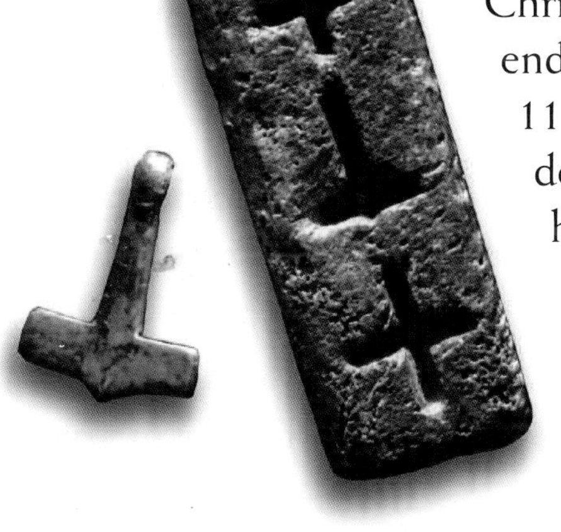

A Viking mold for jewellery shows the Christian cross and Thor's hammer—symbols of the old and new religions.

Glossary

abbot The superior monk in a monastery

berserker An ancient Norse warrior who fought in a wild frenzy

breach A gap in the fortifications or line of defense of an enemy caused by attacking forces

chalice A special cup used in Christian ceremonies

Christianity The religion of Christians, who believe in one God and follow the teachings of Jesus Christ

Domesday Book The manuscript of a vast survey of England and Wales which was ordered by William I and completed in 1086; it documents the value of land and livestock held by landholders

draft How deep water must be for a loaded ship to float

duchy A territory ruled by a duke or duchess; a dukedom

earls An English noble

East Anglia A region of eastern England

fortress A heavily protected and impenetrable building

fryd An Anglo-Saxon militia made up of civilians

heathen A person who does not worship the Christian God

horde A massive group of people

housecarls Members of the bodyguard who protected a Danish or English king or nobleman

Islam The religion of Muslims who follow the teachings of God, whom Muslims call Allah, and his prophet Muhammad

javelin A light spear, thrown as a weapon

Loki A mischievous, and sometimes evil, Norse god

medieval Of the time of or relating to the Middle Ages

mercenaries Soldiers who fight for pay or for plunder they can take rather than out of loyalty or because of commitment to a cause

Muslim A follower of the religion of Islam

noble Belonging by rank, title, or birth to the aristocracy (the upper classes) of a society or civilization

oath A serious promise

Odin The supreme Norse god and creator; god of victory and of the dead; also known as Woden or Wodan by the Anglo-Saxons

pagan A person whose religious beliefs are not those of any of the main world religions, such as Christianity, Judaism, or Islam

palisade A high fence of pointed stakes erected to provide protection

phalanx A group of soldiers who stand or move together in a close, defensive formation

plunder Something of value taken by force or theft

priory A religious house, such as a monastery

prow The bow or front of a ship

rampart A defensive wall of a castle or walled city

relic An object surviving from an earlier time, especially one of historical, holy, or sentimental interest; often the bone of a saint

Roman empire An empire established by Augustus in 27 BCE and divided in 395 CE into western (Latin) and eastern (Greek) empires

stronghold A place that has been strengthened to protect against attack

succession The action or process of inheriting a title such as king

thane A man who traded military service for land in medieval England

Thor Norse god of thunder, the weather, agriculture, and the home; Son of Odin and Freya

Anglo-Saxon noble Hereward the Wake led a strong resistance to the Norman invasion in 1070, and eventually won back his land.

Index